NCC
The National Computing Centre

The National Computing Centre develops techniques and provides aids for the more effective use of computers. NCC is a non-profit-distributing organisation backed by government and industry. The Centre

— co-operates with, and co-ordinates the work of, members and other organisations concerned with computers and their use

— provides information, advice and training

— supplies software packages

— publishes books

— promotes standards and codes of practice

Any interested company, organisation or individual can benefit from the work of the Centre by subscribing as a member. Throughout the country, facilities are provided for members to participate in working parties, study groups and discussions, and to influence NCC policy. A regular journal — 'NCC Interface' — keeps members informed of new developments and NCC activites. Special facilities are offered for courses, training material, publications and software packages.

For further details get in touch with the Centre at Oxford Road, Manchester M1 7ED (telephone 061-228 6333)

or at one of the following regional offices

Belfast	1st Floor 117 Lisburn Road BT9 7BP	Glasgow	2nd Floor, Anderston House Argyle Street G2 8LR
Telephone:	0232 665997		
		Telephone:	041-204 1101
Birmingham	2nd Floor Prudential Buildings Colmore Row B3 2PL	London	11 New Fetter Lane EC4A 1PU
		Telephone:	01-353 4875
Telephone:	021-236 6283		
Bristol	6th Floor Royal Exchange Building 41 Corn Street BS1 1HG		
Telephone:	0272 27077		

Introducing Microprocessors

G. L. Simons

Keywords for information retrieval (drawn from the
NCC Thesaurus of Computing Terms): Microprocessors,
Systems design, Software, Social consequences of computers

British Library Cataloguing in Publication Data

Simons, G L
    Introducing microprocessors.
    1. Microcomputers
    I. Title
    001.6'4044   QA76.5

    ISBN 0-85012-209-0

First published in 1979 by:
NCC Publications, The National Computing Centre Limited,
Oxford Road, Manchester M1 7ED, England

Printed in England by H Charlesworth & Co Ltd, Huddersfield

ISBN 0-85012-209-0

Acknowledgements

I am grateful to David Taylor, NCC Senior Consultant involved in various microprocessor application projects, for reading this book in typescript and for his varied and helpful comments; and to Dr T. D. Wells, also of NCC, for providing information on MODBUS.

Thanks are also due to NCC Information Services for responding so promptly and efficiently, often in difficult circumstances, to my many requests.

Finally I would thank Mrs Edna Taylor, NCC Management Services, for typing to her characteristic high standard the bulk of the first draft.

Disclaimer

There are a few brief comments in Chapter 6 on the attitudes of government and trade unions. The views expressed are the author's and not necessarily those of The National Computing Centre Limited.

Preface

This is an introductory book. In no sense does it aim to be definitive. I am very conscious that there are many microprocessor-models, related chips, and programming languages that are not mentioned here. Similarly there are scores of applications that are not even hinted at. It is impossible to survey the various microprocessor aspects and at the same time to give exhaustive detail.

The aim is to profile the important areas, to highlight key considerations in this rapidly developing field. The book should be set in the context of the veritable explosion of interest in microelectronics, the scale of the new technology, and the accelerating pace of international innovation. The reader is presented with some information, a tiny proportion of what is available in the literature, and some impressions. There is guidance on how to obtain more information.

Some introductory books are safe but superficial. They give a balanced general view with not much detailed information. The present book aims to give some detail in the broad panorama. There are bound to be many omissions, but it is hoped that the profile will be useful.

G L SIMONS
Senior Consultant
Chief Editor, NCC Publications

Contents

1 What is a Microprocessor?

INTRODUCTION

A *microprocessor* is a component in a *microcomputer*. It is the central data processing part, responsible for the fundamental operations of logic and arithmetic upon which all computer intelligence is based. The microprocessor is the functional equivalent of the central processing unit (CPU) in traditional large computers.

Microprocessors are small (the smallest will pass through the eye of a needle). This means that they can be sited in a very wide range of other manufactured equipment. They are cheap to buy, particularly when purchased in quantity; and they are cheap to operate, having very low electrical power requirements.

THE COMPUTER BACKGROUND

The early electronic computers of the 1940s had central processing units built up of banks of vacuum tubes, the 'glass bottles' also found in old wireless sets and television receivers. The CPUs needed thousands of these tubes. The systems were cumbersome and unreliable (only hours between failures). There were heavy electrical power demands, and the cooling plant was often as large as the computer.

The first computer of this type (said with hindsight to be 'first generation') was ENIAC (Electronic Numerical Integrator and Computer), developed in the US by J. P. Eckert and J. W. Mauchly. ENIAC, completed by 1946, was designed with the purpose of generating artillery firing tables. Built up from 18,000 vacuum tubes, it was immense, requiring a room 60ft by 25ft to hold it and weighing more than 30 tons.

In 1948 the transistor was first demonstrated by William Shockley, John Bardeen and Walter Brattain, working in the Bell

Telephone Laboratories in the US. Transistors can do virtually all the jobs of the then-conventional vacuum-tube valves, but require much less electrical power, generate very little heat, and are much smaller. They are also considerably more reliable, and made possible the development of computers as effective functional devices in an increasingly wide range of applications.

The computers of the 1950s and early 1960s individually used thousands of transistors. The various electronic components — transistors, resistors, capacitors, diodes, etc — were mounted on printed-circuit cards (or 'boards'): copper was selectively etched from a phenolic or fibreglass base to leave electrical connections between holes in which the wires of the components were inserted. A typical 5-in square printed-circuit card would contain about a dozen transistors and a hundred or so other components.

Each computer (now 'second generation') comprised several thousand printed-circuit cards. The cards, regarded as modules, were slotted into frames and interconnected by means of back wiring. A typical large computer would be built up from several dozen specific modules, each of them being used up to several hundred times in each computer.

In the 1960s the semiconductor makers created a whole new technology, making possible the development of 'third generation' computers. Using a more sophisticated version of transistor fabrication technology it was possible to manufacture dozens of transistors together on a single small silicon chip. In this way an electronic circuit, previously comprising many separate interconnected components, could be manufactured as a single integrated unit.

Today the basic components — transistors, diodes, etc — can be assembled in a 10 μm-thick surface layer on a silicon wafer. The components are then connected by a metal layer evaporated onto the silicon. Subsequent etching produces the required interconnections. Several of the integrated circuits can be mounted on a printed-circuit card which can now carry all the circuitry necessary for a central processing unit and the associated computer elements.

By the early 1970s, integrated circuits were manufactured with a complexity of around 1000 transistors. The first microprocessor, produced by Intel Corporation in 1971, was based on a single ¼-in-square silicon chip which carried the equivalent of 2250 transistors, all the necessary CPU circuitry for a tiny computer. By 1976, chips of this size using LSI (Large Scale Integration) could carry more than 20,000 components.

When a computer's central processing unit is one integrated circuit, or a small number of ICs, the CPU is termed a microprocessor. A microprocessor is used with other (often integrated) components to form a microcomputer.

MICROCOMPUTER ARCHITECTURE

General

All computers have similar architectural features: a microcomputer has functional elements equivalent to those of a large mainframe. A computer, of whatever size, needs to carry out the operations of logic and arithmetic. It needs storage facilities for program instructions and the numerical quantities involved in computation. It needs a 'bus' system for interconnecting the various functional components, and input/output facilities to allow the computer to interact with the larger system of which it forms a part. And it needs a control facility to organise in time all the necessary operations.

Computers vary in performance (actual or potential) according to various characteristics: storage capacity, the detailed CPU architecture, the number of specific elements interconnected by the bus system, and the particular technological process used to manufacture the various components. Microcomputers, small and innovatory, may be expected to have lower performance – in terms of flexibility, speed, etc – than the larger minicomputers and mainframes. However, microcomputers are encroaching on many applications areas formerly the exclusive province of the larger computers – and this in addition to discovering a vast new range of computer application possibilities.

The architectural features of computers are similar but not identical. The various microcomputer families on the market all exhibit unique architectures: in some instances this distinctive character defines the particular family to which a microcomputer model belongs. In one breakdown of microcomputer types, five basic categories of system are recognised: single-chip microcomputers, 2-chip-set microcomputers, general-purpose microprocessor systems, high-performance microprocessor systems, and bit-slice systems. (Some of these types are self-explanatory; others are described below.) For other purposes, microcomputers are defined according to the technological process used to manufacture the various integrated circuits.

Microcomputers are all made up from similar basic elements, though the design and organisation of these elements differ considerably from one microcomputer model to another. In one simple version (fig. 1.1), the basic elements are: the microprocessor unit, a read-only memory (ROM) to hold the program, a random-access memory (RAM) to hold computation results, the variable-data input/output (I/O) units and the interconnecting buses.

In this version the various elements are interconnected by a data bus and an address bus. The data bus carries data and instructions. The address bus carries a microprocessor output to specify the address of the data or instruction required. The microprocessor is under program control. When an address is specified the stored information is fed along the data bus to the microprocessor unit.

The basic architecture (fig. 1.1) can be extended or modified in various ways. Storage facilities and input/output sections can be enlarged by means of additional integrated circuits. More than one microprocessor unit can share the same storage or memory facilities. An enhanced input/output section can increase the microcomputer's sensitivity to external user demands.

Microprocessor Unit

In most microcomputers the microprocessor unit may be considered to comprise two basic elements: *the arithmetic and logic unit (ALU)* and the *control unit*. In addition to these basic units there may be storage facilities of various types.

The *arithmetic and logic unit* comprises one or more integrated circuits internally organised to define an arrangement of logic gates. These gates, according to their type and how they are organised, accept numerical inputs and then provide outputs specified by program instructions. For example, an instruction specifying a simple addition of two numbers will arrange for each of the numbers to be fed to the appropriate ALU gate inputs. The gates – in this case organised as an *addition* circuit – produce an output which is the result required. The numbers are represented in binary arithmetic (with, for example, the presence of an electrical pulse representing a '1', its absence a '0').

The *control unit* can help to organise the timing of operations within the ALU: to ensure, for example, that the various binary digits arrive at the appropriate gate inputs in the right sequence and at the right time. The operation of the control unit may in turn be governed by a *master clock* which defines the *cycle time* for the microcomputer. The master clock distributes signals,

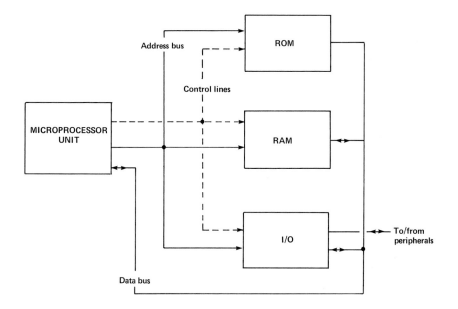

Figure 1.1 Microcomputer Architecture

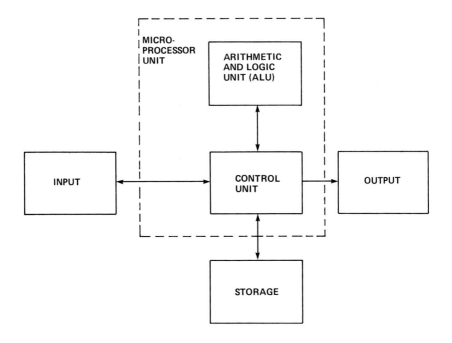

Figure 1.2   Control Routes

usually in the form of square waves, throughout the computer — to the microprocessor unit, storage devices, input/output sections, etc — to coordinate and sequence the various operations.

(The precision of the master clock's reference is relevant to programming considerations. Most clocks are controlled at a fixed frequency by a quartz crystal. In some microcomputers, the clock is controlled by a less-expensive, but much less precise, resistor-capacitor timing circuit. Such circuits, as with the other microcomputer elements, can be obtained as integrated components. Most prefabricated microcomputers and single-board computers use crystals. Many computer-controlled games, not requiring such precise timing, employ simple resistor-capacitor timing circuits.)

A simple block diagram (fig. 1.2) shows the relation of the control unit to other computer elements.

Storage

In any microcomputer it is necessary to *store* program instructions, numbers ('operands') to use in computation, the results of computation, and other items. Sometimes the information is stored permanently, as with instructions; sometimes the storage requirement is temporary, as with particular reference numbers that may be updated or abandoned.

Individual storage locations are assigned unique identifying numbers ('addresses'). Data for use in computation can be written into or read out of memory by addressing particular storage locations. The amount of memory a particular microcomputer can work with is determined by the number of address lines controlled by the microprocessor unit. Most current processors have sixteen address lines which can be used to identify 2^{16} memory locations, ie the microcomputer can operate with 65,536 items ('words') of memory. In some cases the amount of memory is limited by hardware availability; in others, by power supply characteristics.

The storage facilities can be of several types: RAM (random-access memory), ROM (read-only memory), PROM (programmable read-only memory), EPROM (erasable programmable read-only memory), etc.

RAMs were developed, at least in part, to overcome the disadvantages of the traditional *shift registers.* Shift registers, simply viewed, consist of a row of circuit elements, each of which can hold a binary 1 or 0. When the appropriate control signals are applied, each element can convey its contents to the next in line. In this way, the last element progressively transfers ('shifts') the full contents of the register onto an output line.

These registers, in common with a wide range of other storage devices, can be built using integrated circuit technology. Only the input to the first element, the output from the last, and a wire for the clock control need to be brought out to the edge of the chip surface. The connections between elements are made during chip manufacture.

Shift registers are *static* or *dynamic.* Elements in a static register preserve data in the absence of a clock signal. Dynamic registers employ a storage medium in which data decays with time. The data is regenerated if shifted soon enough along the register. Dynamic devices require less space than their static equivalent, and also use less power. The clear disadvantage of dynamic devices is that the contents of a register must be shifted frequently, whether or not they are required that often for computation, just to preserve them. Both static and dynamic shift registers lose their contents when power is removed, so where necessary a back-up power supply is included in system design.

These devices are suitable for various applications. They can, for example, be used for refreshing a raster-scan CRT display, where data moves serially to and from memory. In many application areas they are less suitable. A typical 1024-bit shift register has a maximum clock frequency of around 10 MHz. This means that it takes about 102 microseconds to convey all the binary digits through the register. The average time to access any particular bit would be about 50 microseconds: this is too slow for many important applications, eg referencing program data. Registers of other sorts, ie ones not relying on a serial shift function, are used throughout the computer architecture for a variety of purposes.

Random-access memory (RAM) devices overcome the data-transfer delay inherent in the traditional shift register. It is also possible to do without the support logic necessary for shift register operation.

In RAM devices, the individual elements used to carry the binary digits are arranged in rows and columns. A separate input (the 'address') has two parts, one to specify a row and one to specify a column. This allows identification of an array element for reading or writing purposes. RAM storage arrays are usually square, so memory sizes usually increase by factors of four:

doubling the number of rows usually goes with a doubling of the number of columns. As with shift registers, the individual storage elements may be dynamic or static.

Static devices are addressed only when data is read or written. With dynamic devices it is essential that the entire RAM be refreshed frequently. Typically, in a 4096-bit dynamic RAM with 64 rows and 64 columns, one row must be refreshed every 31 microseconds. The refresh circuitry can be shared by all the memory chips in the computer. In large memory systems the refresh circuitry costs are relatively small.

Static RAMs are commonly available with 1024- and 4096-bit capacities. Dynamic RAMs are available in sizes up to 16K. In general, the faster a device, the more power it consumes. Power consumption also varies according to the particular technology on which the device is based: NMOS devices consume more power than do CMOS devices (see below). RAMs lose their contents when the power is switched off (or through power failure). Programs and other fixed data must be stored elsewhere, then copied into RAMs as needed.

Read-only memories (ROMs) retain data when power disappears, ie they are non-volatile, but they sacrifice writability. An ROM is usually written once, when manufactured, and then read repeatedly thereafter. A blank memory is fabricated using standard semiconductor manufacturing techniques. Then a 'bit mask' is employed to set the memory elements to certain binary values. Typical mask-programmed ROMs have 32K and 64K capacities, making ROMs much cheaper than RAMs. Where programs are encapsulated in ROM devices, program changes (including debugging) are impossible. However, these devices are very suitable for high-volume applications such as products for the consumer market.

Programmable read-only memories (PROMs) are an alternative to ROMs in circumstances where production volumes (or the possibility of error) do not warrant the use of mask-programmed devices. Each bit element in the PROM contains a 'fuse' which can be 'blown' by means of an appropriate programming instruction. An element with an unblown fuse reads out a 1; with a blown fuse, a 0. As may be expected, PROMs are more expensive than ROMs, but they can be programmed for a particular purpose within minutes.

Manual PROM programmers are prone to error. It is more effective to connect a PROM programmer to a microcomputer.

This enables the operator to copy validated programs directly from the computer's RAM into a PROM. Data can be read back and compared with the original RAM contents to confirm that all the required fuses have been blown. If necessary, the PROM can be reprogrammed, though clearly a wrongly blown fuse cannot be corrected.

PROMs are capable of high speeds, important in computer applications requiring microprogram storage. They consume a lot of power but, since they are non-volatile, can be switched off when not being accessed.

Erasable programmable read-only memories (EPROMs) can be erased by exposure to intense ultraviolet light (termed 'UV-erasable'); other ROMs are electrically-alterable (termed 'EAROMs'). Reading takes place more often than writing, so erasable PROMs generally have read-access times less than 500 nanoseconds, with writing and erasing taking longer. In some systems a UV erasing lamp is installed in the memory subsystem. Usually, however, EPROMs are removed before being erased.

In real-time applications it is convenient electrically to erase and write data into a non-volatile memory. EAROMs from General Instruments, Nitron, NEC Microsystems and other companies allow this to be done. EAROMs are competitive with EPROMs, following similar pricing policies. EAROMs can often be used as substitutes for UV-EPROMs, with the advantage that data can be copied from RAMs into non-volatile storage without resorting to UV lamps. EAROMs are also easier to deal with when debugging is required.

Increasing attention is being given to integrated memories based on *magnetic bubble* technology and on *charge-coupled* technology. In the bubble memory, essentially a shift register, each individual memory element is carried on a sheet of specially-prepared rare-earth material. These memories are intended as bulk stores, cheap to manufacture but with lengthy average access time. Bubble memory is seen as filling the gap between fast but volatile semiconductor RAM and rotating mass storage devices. Charge-coupled devices (CCD) are also essentially shift registers, seen as rivalling disks and drums as mass storage media. CCDs are faster than bubble memories but are volatile.

Buses

Microcomputers, in common with minicomputers and large mainframes, have a *bus structure* (ie a system of electrical interconnections) to carry the data, control and address information to the various parts of the computer. In general the bus (or buses, according to linguistic convention) links modules within the computer system and also links the microcomputer to other devices. Some computers use a (*de facto*) standard bus arrangement. This means that a memory board, for example, can be taken from computer X and plugged in to computer Y. Standard buses are compatible with boards from different manufacturers.

The bus structure adopted for a particular microprocessor-based system determines its interface capability, and helps to define its performance. The bus structure within the microcomputer helps to define the size of data word that can be handled and the speed at which processing can take place. The external bus structure allows the microcomputer to interface with other devices.

Buses, of whatever type, may be regarded as effective communication channels. Various types of information are transmitted between the various components of a microcomputer: program and data-memory addresses, instruction codes, data to and from memory, input/output addresses, and data to and from the I/O devices. In a large computer there is likely to be a bus unique to the type of information, but in a microcomputer system, differing types of information may be carried, under appropriate timing control, on the same bus. A typical microcomputer might have only two buses — one shared by the instruction codes and data from memory, and one by the program and data-memory address. An element of sharing is necessary because of the limited number of pins on the standard integrated circuit package.

Shared bus structures can be either *daisy-chain* or *party-line*. In a daisy-chain arrangement, the information passes through each system component along a loop of unidirectional buses until it arrives at the correct device. Each component serves as both a source and acceptor of information on the bus. In party-line structures, each component is linked directly to a single bus. This type of structure is consistent with either a unidirectional or a bidirectional bus. Most microcomputers employ a bidirectional party-line structure for the main data bus, but the structure of other buses differs from one computer model (and application) to another.

Two particular buses are regarded as *de facto* standards though without some of the advantages of formal definition: the S-100 bus and the SS-50 bus. The S-100 (Altair/IMSAI/Processor Tech/ Poly 88/etc) is used in most 8080 and Z80 systems. The SS-50

(Southwest Technical Products/Midwest Scientific Instruments/ Gimix/etc) is used by 6800 processors. The most popular bus configuration is the S-100, which allows the adding of memory, interface ports, battery back-up boards, music system boards, etc, simply by plugging in the appropriate circuit boards. The SS-50 (with 50 pins rather than 100) appears to be increasing in popularity. Other popular buses are LSI-11 (which derived from DEC experience with UNIBUS), MULTIBUS (promulgated by Intel), IEEE 488 (for instrument designers), and SBC-80 (for a range of single-board computers).

Different bus systems can be linked together by means of an electrical interface. In such circumstances the combined system has to operate at the speed of the slower bus. It can be advantageous to link buses: for example, an S-100/MULTIBUS interface would enable MULTIBUS systems to use the broad range of memory and peripheral controller cards available for use with S-100. However, S-100 peripherals can be adapted for use with MULTIBUS, and no manufacturer has yet produced a standard S-100/MULTIBUS interface card.

There are more than 400 cards available from more than 100 manufacturers for S-100. This bus, *de facto* standard that it represents, is defined well enough to enable most modules to work together. However, undefined features restrict the possibility of innovation. For example, a computer introduced on an S-100-compatible card would be constrained to operate at Altair 8800 speeds to ensure compatibility with other cards on the market. In this case it is arguable that absence of a fully-defined bus standard prevents adoption of the latest technology.

National Semiconductor Corporation has designed a component-level 'standard' called Microbus — to define a general-purpose microprocessor interface that will ensure integrated circuit compatibility with present and future microprocessor systems; to provide the user with a means of interconnecting independently manufactured devices into a single system; to define a bus that restricts device performance as little as possible; and to define fully an easy-to-use bus system.

Microbus is intended for all microprocessor-based systems using 8-bit parallel transfer of digital data between the microprocessor and the devices with which it interfaces. A unified bus system is provided for linking components in close proximity to one another. It can be used with systems comprising fewer than 10 integrated circuits connected to a common bus. Microbus attempts to steer a middle course between the needs of standardisation and those of technological innovation, and to aid design of micro-processor-based systems.

The IEEE 488 Bus, known also as general-purpose interface bus (GP-1B) or the Hewlett-Packard Interface Bus (HP-IB), has been approved by the International Electrotechnical Commission. This prepares the way for a worldwide standard for interconnect systems. The IEEE 48 Bus is now being referred to as the 'micro-computer interconnect system of the future'.

In the United Kingdom the Ministry of Defence has produced specifications for a MODBUS/EUROBUS system. Specifically EUROBUS is a shelf-based interface occupying one connector of a Double Eurocard, leaving the other free for input-output con-nections. All aspects of bus operation are fully handshaken allowing devices of differing response speed to be connected together. Of particular interest is the fact that specifications in this area are unlikely to stop at the card/bus level but may extend to frame structures and power distribution methods – in short an engineered solution for professional applications. Developments based around the bus are in early stages but it is attracting interest outside the defence field (the SPS division of CERN has specified it for use as a manufacturer-independent interface). For commercial applica-tions, Ferranti Ltd, Bracknell, sell copies of the specification, the rights to which are, however, MOD-owned.

Input/Output

Communication with the microcomputer is essential: it is worth-less if it cannot talk to the larger system or to the user. The various processes and equipment associated with getting informa-tion into and out of the computer are called I/O (input/output). This usually involves such devices as a keyboard, a TV monitor, or a printer. CRT terminals are useful in this context, having both a keyboard and a TV monitor as well as the necessary interface circuitry.

The I/O facilities of a microcomputer may be regarded as comprising *input/output ports* and *interface circuits*. The I/O ports comprise the circuitry used to detect or initiate inputs and outputs. The interface circuits are used to convert the logic signals to and from the kinds of voltages and currents required by the larger system. The I/O ports and interface circuits can often be bought 'off-the-shelf' but many computer applications require specially designed interfaces.

The ports and interfaces can be designed for either *serial* or *parallel* operation. In a serial port, normally used with CRT terminals, the bits of data all move along the same line, one after the other. (Two electrical standards for serial operation are the RS-232 voltage level standard and the 20 ma current loop.) Serial ports are often linked to telephone lines or used with terminals designed for connection to telephone lines. Most local data transfers are handled via parallel ports.

In parallel operation, the bits of information move along parallel lines at the same time, not sequentially. Parallel ports, able to transfer all the bits of a data word simultaneously, are generally used for printers and keyboard inputs. It is possible to transfer single bits of data via a parallel port.

The same type of integrated circuit can be used for both the input and output sides of the port. Different control signals initiate the required activities. In a typical port, an 8-bit-wide register is used to hold output data, and an 8-bit-wide three-state buffer allows input data to be selectively transferred to the data line. The I/O integrated circuits have parallel input and output paths, and five discrete control signals. The I/O module responds to addresses presented during the times which permit an I/O read or an I/O write operation. The read and write times are determined by specific control signals.

Some computers have one set of signals for reading or writing memory and another set for reading or writing I/O ports. Other computers use only one set of control signals for these purposes. Traditionally, but without intrinsic reason, computers have separated I/O transactions from memory data transfers. Some microcomputers, eg the Motorola 6800, do not have input/output instructions.

Input/output devices often operate independently of the rest of the microcomputer. In these circumstances it is necessary to synchronise program execution with I/O device operation when data is transmitted. I/O data transfers can be *program-controlled, interrupt-controlled,* or controlled through *direct-memory-access.* The approach adopted depends on the required rate of data transmission, the maximum acceptable time delay between the I/O device indicating readiness to transmit or receive data and the actual data transfer, and the feasibility of interleaving I/O operations with other microcomputer activity.

With program-controlled I/O, the computer's input/output instructions initiate and control all types of data transfer. Control data are used to synchronise the I/O device with program execution. There are various ways of organising the I/O program instructions. For example, a unique instruction can be allocated to each type of data transfer; or two instructions — one for input and one for output — can be provided to transfer all required data ('message' and control).

A simple version of interrupt control involves a single I/O device connected to an interrupt-request line. A signal on this line causes an automatic move from the main program to a predetermined location in program memory. When the interrupt sequence has been completed, a return is made to the main program. A second interrupt cannot take place while the interrupt sequence is being performed.

Various types of interrupt control are available. There may be enhanced provision for retaining the contents of important registers or microcomputer architecture may be designed specifically to facilitate interrupts. Some microcomputers use locations in data memory instead of the usual internal registers. In some applications it is useful to employ a real-time clock (eg a high-frequency oscillator) to provide regular signals on the interrupt-request line. And there are circumstances when it is necessary to handle multiple interrupts. This can be done on a priority basis. The more flexible the interrupt facility the more complex the I/O circuitry. For example, additional registers will be required to allow an accurate return to main program: it is necessary to store, usually on a temporary basis, details of the various interrupt requests being serviced.

Sometimes, required data transfer is too rapid for effective I/O control by the microprocessor. In such cases, data must travel directly between the I/O device and the microcomputer memory. This is achieved by means of a direct-memory-access (DMA) facility.

Data transfer is controlled by a DMA logic circuit that can operate faster than the microprocessor. The DMA controller effectively takes over the microprocessor memory. An external control line may be used to stop the microprocessor at a particular point in the main program. Or the microcomputer clock may be halted, allowing the DMA controller to 'steal' several cycles of microcomputer operation.

Effective input/output operation is essential in all microcomputer applications. For many purposes it is possible to regard the microcomputer as a functional 'black box', but for it to be useful we, or the larger system in which it is a component, have to be able to instruct it and to receive the correct response.

Bit-sliced Architecture

Some architectural features help to define families of microcomputers. *Bit-sliced* architecture, for example, is a defining characteristic of a whole range of microprocessor-based products. It is usually contrasted with single-chip architecture.

Single-chip microprocessors have become increasingly popular in recent years. They are extremely small and cheap, and in many applications have replaced conventional hardwired or random logic with programmable logic. A major disadvantage of MOS-based (see Technology below) devices is their relatively slow speed. This has confined them to applications not needing high execution rates.

Bit-sliced microprocessors (using bipolar technology), by contrast, enhance system flexibility and increase speeds by a factor of 10. Bit-sliced devices differ from single-chip (MOS) microprocessors mainly in their CPU architecture. In single-chip microprocessors, the data processing function and the control function are both hardwired on the same chip, whereas in bit-sliced bipolar devices these two CPU functions are allocated separate chips. Single-chip processors have fixed word length, architecture and instruction sets. Bit-sliced systems can be configured for different architectures, word lengths and instruction-set capabilities.

The first bit-slice microprocessor was produced in 1974, by Monolithic Memories Inc. This was the 4-bit-wide 6701 processor element, marketed as a microcontroller. No support circuits or design aids were offered. In 1974 and 1975, Intel and Advanced Micro Devices introduced families of bipolar LSI microprocessors, to be followed soon by products from other manufacturers.

There are currently six families of bit-slice microprogrammable processor sets: the 6701/67110 (Monolithic Memories), the 3000 series (Intel), the 2900 series (Advanced Micro Devices), the Macrologic series (Fairchild), the 74S481/82 and SBP0400 (Texas Instruments) and the 10800 series (Motorola). The parts are marketed as families of devices that are to be used together to implement a processor.

With a bit-sliced architecture, the instruction set can be defined by a program stored in a PROM. Architecture and processing capability can be adapted to the requirements of the application. Furthermore, the final system is more flexible: a few macroinstructions, or the PROM that holds them, can be changed. These facilities require significant investment in support software, and working with bit-sliced microprocessors can be more difficult than working with single-chip processors. The designer is required to have an appropriate mix of hardware and software skills.

The microprogrammable CPU in a bit-sliced architecture is implemented on a multi-chip basis. This is because of current limitations on chip complexity, pin numbers, and chip size feasible with bipolar technologies.

The *control* section, allocated one chip, is generally more complex than the *processing* section, allocated another. The control section defines the machine's instruction set and comprises microprogram memory, a microprogram-sequencer, and other circuitry such as selection logic and registers. The memory holds the instructions which govern the machine processes and which control the parallel operation of the RALU (register arithmetic logic unit) slices of the processing section. The sequencer ensures that the microprograms are effective in the correct order.

The processing section comprises functionally-equivalent chips, the bit-slices or RALUs, each containing registers, an arithmetic-logic unit, and other circuitry. Most bipolar microprocessors are built using 2-bit or 4-bit slices, operating in parallel and accumulated to any width that is a multiple of the basic slice. This allows design of microprocessors that can handle non-conventional word lengths (eg 24, 32 and 48 bits).

Microprograms are now used to operate aggregates of processor slices in parallel. User microprogrammability and bit-sliced architectures allow the system designer to work in a new dimension to meet special applications requirements. There is also scope for using the microprogramming approach in non-CPU applications. Bipolar LSI memories, inexpensive and fast, can be used with microprogramming techniques in a wide range of digital systems.

When bipolar bit-slice processors first emerged on the market, they were almost totally unsupported by other circuits and design aids. Now the situation has changed and it is sometimes difficult for potential users to find their way through the proliferation of products.

THE DEVELOPMENT OF MICROPROCESSORS

The first microprocessor, Intel's 4004, was a 4-bit device having broadly the same computational ability as the 1946 glass-valve

ENIAC.

In 1969, Busicom, a Japanese company contracted with Intel to develop integrated circuits for a printer-calculator. The result was a chip set that used a 4-bit data bus and four integrated circuits: a central processing unit, a read only memory with I/O, a programmable memory with I/O, and a shift register. Intel was allowed to market the device in non-calculator applications, whereupon the first generation of microprocessors was developed.

The 4004 processor chip would only interface with other chips in the family. Since programs could only be executed out of read-only memory, and since programmable memory was used only to store data, it was difficult to debug software. Also, a considerable amount of support logic was required.

In 1972, following involvement with Datapoint, Intel produced the 8008, an 8-bit microprocessor. This was a more general-purpose device than the 4004, having an instruction set similar to a mini-computer's, interrupt capability, and the capacity to address directly 16K bytes of programmable memory. With the 8008 microprocessor and Intel's 1101 and 1702 integrated-circuit memories, it was possible to build general-purpose microcomputers.

The 8008 was followed, a year later, by Intel's 8080, an 8-bit device which operated at 20 times the speed of the 8008. The new 8080 became the first *de facto* industry standard, used in more applications than any other processor.

In 1974, Motorola introduced the 8-bit 6800 microprocessor. Compared with the 8080, the 6800 had a simplified power supply, simpler control circuitry, and instructions more compatible with larger computers. This microprocessor, with programmable input/output facilities, was to become the second *de facto* industry standard.

Intel and Motorola both announced 'true single-chip processors' in 1976, by which time many other companies were making important contributions. National Semiconductor had introduced the IMP-16 chip set in 1972, a bit-slice system that developed into the Pace microprocessor. 1975 and 1976 saw the emergence of a number of enhanced systems. The Zilog Z80 was an enhanced 8080, with more instructions and registers, a one-chip clock and other features.

The first 16-bit microprocessors also emerged at this time, with 4-bit and 8-bit devices continuing to evolve for particular purposes.

The first widely-available 16-bit devices were the TMS9900 and TMS9980 from Texas Instruments. Such microprocessors could multiply and divide, unlike many of their 8-bit contemporaries.

The earliest microcomputers were slow and relatively inflexible. Their storage capacity was low and there were software problems. However, new technological developments added speed and storage capacity, and enhanced the applications flexibility. Today, in 1979, some *micro*computers are offering *mini*computer performance levels. 16-bit microprocessors such as the Intel 8086, the Motorola MC68000 and the Zilog Z8000 offer large address spaces, wide data paths, and speeds of more than 500,000 instructions per second. Since 1971, microprocessor complexity has doubled every two years.

Intel's relatively new 8086 has brought the 8080 family of microprocessors into the 16-bit world. The new device has enhanced capabilities and new peripheral support circuits (clock generator, bus controller, etc). It has been designed to meet the requirements of a broad class of new applications. Similarly, the Motorola MC68000 has been designed with greater capability and enhanced peripheral support. Its internal data paths, registers and processing sections are 32-bits wide. Support peripherals include a memory manager, a direct-memory-access controller, and a bus arbitration circuit. The Z8000 is accompanied by a whole new family of peripheral chips.

One of the most significant development areas in microprocessor technology is the provision of support chips. This was well shown at Wescon (1978) where a wide variety of new products were exhibited (American Microsystems S2811 signal processing peripheral, TRW high-speed multipliers, semicustom logic arrays from Fairchild and Motorola, etc). These and parallel developments indicate that microcomputers will continue to grow in capability, enlarging their applications potential, and offering alternatives to conventional minicomputer (and even mainframe) usage.

THE TECHNOLOGIES OF COMPUTERS

General

The circuitry for computers (microcomputers, minis, mainframes) is built out of standard families of integrated circuits. The various integrated-circuit devices — counters, registers, adders, etc — are combined according to a theoretical design to perform the required functions. There are various *semiconductor technologies* upon which the families of integrated circuits are based.

Most computer circuits in use today are based on *transistor-transistor* logic (TTL). This technology is common, a virtual standard, in large computers, but considerably less popular in microcomputers. A very wide range of devices are available in TTL from many manufacturers. TTL has been the most popular logic family for more than a decade: it provides high speed, high immunity to noise, moderate power dissipation, and large 'fan-out' (ie TTL devices can drive a large number of other circuit components). Other integrated-circuit families are often judged according to how well their devices can interface with TTL. Non-TTL devices that use signal levels within the range of standard transistor-transistor logic are termed 'TTL-compatible'.

There are two variations on standard TTL: Schottky (54/74 S) and low-power Schottky (54/74 LS). The Schottky variant can provide higher speed than standard TTL. Lower power dissipation is possible with low-power Schottky. Both these variants are more expensive than standard devices.

Transistor-transistor logic was first produced by Sylvania in 1965, with Texas 7400 TTL becoming the effective industry standard logic in 1968. A year later, *metal-oxide semiconductor* (MOS) technology was first used in the manufacture of large-scale integrated (LSI) circuits. MOS technology (sometimes regarded as *metal-oxide silicon*) is the basis for most current memory chips and microprocessors. Some TTL LSI devices are available (eg the Ferranti F100-L microprocessor).

Devices based on MOS technology represent the second largest family of circuit elements. The *complementary metal-oxide semiconductor* (CMOS) process produces components that are more expensive and slower than ones based on TTL. At the same time they are more rugged and use less power, being suitable for a wide range of applications: industrial, military, portable equipment, domestic (eg watches), etc. They are useful in artificial satellites where low power dissipation is important. CMOS elements can be damaged by static charges.

Some high-speed (and high-cost) CMOS devices use an insulating sapphire substrate. This technique is termed *silicon-on-sapphire* (SOS), a technology which offers potential for very large-scale integration (VLSI) but which has failed in some production attempts (eg the now withdrawn GA processor manufactured by Rockwell). It is likely that cost savings will be achieved in SOS circuit manufacture using new techniques. RCA is developing a method of growing sapphire substrates for integrated circuits in ribbons instead of in cylindrical boules. This is expected to cut the cost of raw materials for silicon-on-sapphire CMOS by around 80%. This will allow CMOS circuits built on bulk silicon wafers to challenge NMOS devices (see below). Hewlett-Packard, already using CMOS/SOS in a range of computer products, is also considering the effectiveness of ribbon-grown sapphire crystals.

Emitter-coupled logic (ECL) is the only other widely-used technology for computer circuits. It is used in mainframes, high-speed memories, precision instruments, and high-speed communications equipment. ECL is expensive and heavy on power consumption. It requires special circuit boards and carefully regulated supplies. ECL families are small and lack standardisation. It is difficult to mix ECL with either TTL or CMOS. ECL circuits have been enhanced with 'gate arrays' (or uncommitted logic arrays, ULA) uncommitted sets of LSI functions tailored by the final metalization to particular applications.

Microprocessors

Neither TTL nor CMOS techniques are ideally suited to meeting the requirements of cheap, single-chip microprocessors, though microprocessors in both these technologies are now available. Most microprocessors are based on either the P-channel or the N-channel metal oxide semiconductor technologies (PMOS and NMOS). In using single-chip microprocessors, it is often required to interface PMOS and NMOS devices to standard TTL and CMOS circuits.

P-channel metal oxide semiconductor (PMOS) technology was the first MOS technology for LSI purposes. It is used in calculator chips and in other applications that do not require high speed. PMOS, though allowing only slow operation, does provide the circuit density essential in large integrated memories and single-chip microprocessors. PMOS components are not strictly TTL-compatible, ie they do not operate at TTL voltages and they provide small output current. Thus additional circuits are necessary to allow PMOS microprocessors to be used with devices from the standard TTL families. Common PMOS microprocessors are the Intel 4004, 4040 and 8008; the National IMP, PACE and SC/MP; the Texas Instruments TMS 1000 NC; and the American Micro-Systems 9209.

N-channel metal oxide semiconductor (NMOS) technology has proved a more suitable basis than PMOS for microprocessor models. It allows higher speed and great density of integrated elements. With some extra circuitry, NMOS devices can operate with TTL components. Common NMOS microprocessors are the Intel 8080, the Motorola 6800, the Fairchild F-8 and the Texas Instruments 9900. NMOS is the most popular microprocessor technology. TTL and ECL microprocessors, relatively uncommon, are used where high-speed operation is required.

Integrated-injection logic (I^2L) is being developed as a relatively new microprocessor technology. It was conceived as allowing high speed and high integration density, at the same time having low power requirements. The future of I^2L technology is uncertain: there is only limited compatibility with other technologies. An example of an I^2L microprocessor is the Texas Instruments SBP 0400.

NMOS microprocessors, with fast access to associated memories and with fast cycle times, will continue to predominate. The problem of interfacing to circuits based on other technologies is likely to persist. There will be more special interface devices, more on-chip interfacing functions, and further efforts to combine technologies on a single substrate. Other technologies may become relevant (eg electron beam lithography).

SUMMARY

Microcomputers, based on microprocessors as central 'computing elements', became feasible with the development of integrated circuits. It became possible to combine the equivalent of thousands of electronic components on a silicon chip. All computers, of whatever size, are built up out of similar functional elements — arithmetic-logic unit, memories, registers, buses, etc. Microcomputers, in common with their larger ancestors and contemporaries, store instructions in a program memory to enable particular functions to be carried out. The semiconductor integrated circuits, used as the basic components in modern computers, are based on several distinct 'technologies' which influence the methods of manufacture and the performance characteristics of the resulting components.

2 Models and Specifications

INTRODUCTION

It is quite impossible to give a detailed and exhaustive description of microprocessors and microprocessor-based products in a single chapter (or, for that matter, in a single book). The last few years have seen an explosive market situation. We are now faced with dozens of commercial microprocessors, hundreds of microcomputers, and thousands of micro-related products. New devices are announced every week, and even journal articles, let alone books, tend to be out-of-date before publication.

Another problem is the question of definition. The speed of technological change has tended to blur the facile distinctions between microcomputers and minicomputers. In the product ranges of some manufacturers there are micros at one end and minis at the other. The various products are broadly compatible but the ranges have a 'grey' area in which the manufactured items may be regarded as micros for some purposes and as minis for others.

The problems of definition and classification are highlighted in the literature. Sometimes (as, for example, in the comprehensive Mostek charts), an attempt is made to give specifications of microprocessor-based products without reference to minicomputers. In other cases (as in the *Datamation* tables), specifications are listed together for microcomputers and minicomputers: 'what appears are general-purpose CPU's available in minimal operating form (with control panel, power supply, and at least 4K of internal memory) at a single-unit end user price of $40,000 or less' (August 1978).

Microcomputers can be configured in various ways. It is even possible to cram an entire microcomputer into a single silicon chip, as with the Motorola 6801. National Semiconductor's SC/MP device needs only one external component − a crystal to control the timing circuit.

Microcomputers are commonly single-board devices using integrated-circuit chips for the various system components; or they may be boxed systems with control panels, keyboards, integrated displays, floppy disk drives, etc. In the various types of microcomputer the microprocessor is usually a single chip, but this is not always so: the CPU of the Motorola MC 10800, for example, comprises three chips. The simplest microcomputers can be purchased for less than £100, with more complex systems costing up to £10,000.

This chapter aims to give an impression of the microcomputer product field. No attempt is made to present exhaustive information on manufacturers or products. Some important products are described in detail: there is no doubt about the impact of certain microprocessors from, say, Intel and Motorola. Attention is also given to products of less significance. In this way, a relatively superficial insight is given into the current market scene.

Sources of further information are indicated, and additional product details are included in Chapter 5.

BACKGROUND

The microprocessor was originally developed by Fairchild for aerospace and defence applications. It was launched as a commercial device by Intel in 1972. Other semiconductor manufacturers – in the US and then in Europe and Japan – followed suit, and today about forty microprocessor suppliers compete in a rapidly expanding market.

Effective industry standards have been established by Intel (with the 8080 device) and Motorola (with the 6800). Intel has maintained its prominence since 1972, now maintaining more than 50 per cent of the world market. In addition to being an effective commercial standard, the 8080 device is listed by the US Defence Department as a 'military standard' product for procurement purposes. Motorola, with the 6800, has captured some 20 to 30 per cent of the market. Many other manufacturers have launched popular competing designs, such as Rockwell (PPS family) and National Semiconductor (SC/MP). Minicomputer manufacturers (Digital Equipment and Data General) have manufactured microprocessors for in-house use, and traditional mainframe makers – IBM, Honeywell (with General Instrument Microelectronics), and Ferranti – have done the same. (Again, care should be taken with terminology: there is now reference to 'mainframe micros', to distinguish them from single-chip micro-computers and single-board systems.)

Available microcomputers are distinguished by their configuration (single-chip, single-board, boxed, etc), by their technology (see Chapter 1), by their compatibility with other devices, by the size of the data word they can handle, and by other factors. The earliest micros could only handle data words comprising four binary digits: a typical 4-bit microprocessor was the Intel 4004. Today, such micros are confined to the simplest control functions (for example, in petrol pumps). The 8-bit word is generally seen as the most convenient, and the vast majority of current micro-processors are 8-bit devices. Some manufacturers – GIM, Ferranti, Plessey and Texas Instruments – have produced powerful 16-bit microprocessors. Intel's 8086 was the first 16-bit micro in the 8080 range, and the Motorola MC 68000 even includes 32-bit wide data paths, registers and processing regions.

Microcomputers also vary in the number of instructions available to the programmer and in other facilities relevant to functional application. Zilog's Z80 can cope with 158 instructions whereas the Rockwell PPS4/Z has only 50. Superficially, one instruction set may seem more powerful than another, but the potential user must take into account such factors as how many program steps are needed to execute a function and what functions can be performed automatically without the need to specify an instruction.

With Direct Memory Access (DMA), data can be read to or from memory without any intervention by the CPU which is allowed thereby to continue with main program execution. Some micro-processors – such as the Intel 8080, the Ferranti F100-L and the Fairchild F8 – offer a DMA facility. This is relevant to flexibility and speed of operation.

The operation of microcomputers, of whatever type, is broadly the same. (In fact a general description applies to the operation of all computers.) The necessary program (ie a set of instructions) is loaded into store. The program counter is set to zero, then incremented, by the clock pulse, to the first program address. The address is fed onto the address bus to cause the contents of the address specified to be fed onto the data bus for delivery to the instruction decoder of the CPU. The instruction, after decoding, is performed by the arithmetic-logic unit, with the results stored as required. The next clock pulse increments the program counter, and the cycle is repeated.

The differences in operation, from one microcomputer to

another, are determined by variations in architecture, basic technology, instruction set, storage capacity, etc. These variations are
depicted in the listed specifications of the different models.

SPECIFICATIONS

Every microprocessor and microcomputer can be defined according
to size, storage capacity, word length, power requirements, instruction set, system compatibility and other features. Specifications appear in the manufacturers' literature, journal articles, wall
charts, etc. The information provided enables potential users to
compare various devices, to assess their suitability for particular
applications.

There is no general agreement as to what a micro specification
should contain. Some specifications provide information on
physical dimensions, suitable environmental conditions, and prices
for individual and bulk purchase; whereas other listings ignore
such features. Some specifications may be detailed in the sense
that they expand on characteristics presented superficially elsewhere. Or they may focus on device features of particular interest
to a definable readership − of, say, an engineering or hobby
journal.

Many journal articles are individually devoted to particular
micro products (see bibliography, Chapter 2). Specifications given
in this context may or may not accord in format and detail with
specifications appearing elsewhere in the same journal or in other
publications. In such cases, in the absence of formalised comparisons, it is up to the potential users to focus on parameters of
interest, and to make comparisons as best they can. Comparisons
may be made on the basis of various features (eg performance
characteristics such as cycle time, memory addressing facilities
and instruction set). In systems based on a complex of microprocessors, the absolute performance of individual processing
elements may not be the most important consideration. Software
or peripheral availability may be more significant factors.

In selecting micro devices it may be necessary to consider
details that do not appear in any specification. For example − has
the device a proven operational record? Is it in volume production?
Does the manufacturer intend further development? Do 'second
sources' of the product exist?

Typical specifications − in brochures, articles, charts, etc −
contain discrete items of information under specific headings.
The headings may be broad (eg 'hardware', 'software', 'peri-

pherals') or specific (eg the word 'hardware' may not appear, detailed attention being given to, say, the 'keyboard', the 'video display unit' and other hardware items). A general description may be given of 'software', or specific information may be given of the 'BASIC interpreter' (eg that it is upward expansible from standard BASIC language and that there are facilities for floating point arithmetic).

Price information may relate to one-off purchase, quantity purchase, and supporting literature (eg an introductory booklet may cost £1, a users' handbook £5). Separate prices may be given for associated peripheral equipment. In some instances manufacturers are reluctant to state prices until they know precisely the character of the intended configuration. Price information may be left out of some comparison charts, potential users being invited to contact the manufacturers.

It is useful to compare a number of specification listings. This indicates the various ways of compiling information on microprocessors and microcomputers. The references, some of which are repeated in the bibliography, also serve as useful specifications of available products. It is important to note that in this rapidly changing field any listing of more than a few months old should be treated with caution. Manufacturers must be regarded as the key sources of information. By way of example, and for the detailed information they contain, seven specification listings are cited (they should be regarded as supplementing manufacturers' brochures, manuals and other published material):

— *Microprocessors,* February 1978 (pp 15–19): listed specifications for 4-, 8-, 12- and 16-bit microcomputers. Attention is given to both US and European products.

— *Microprocessors,* April 1978 (pp 96–101): comparison charts for Intel 8048, Rockwell R6500 and Intersil 6100.

— *Computer Products International,* May 1978 (pp 10–13): listed specifications for 4-, 8-, and 16-bit devices. Price information is included for one-off and quantity purchase.

— *Datamation,* August 1978 (pp 116–118, 120, 122–123, 126): listed specifications for a wide range of microcomputers and minicomputers. Figures are included for numbers shipped (where details are available).

— *Electronic Design,* 11/10/78 (90 pp): detailed information to help potential users to evaluate micro products from more than thirty manufacturers. The main section includes a data page for each microprocessor or family of processors. (At the time of publication of the present book, ie May 1979, the price information is nearly a year out-of-date.)

- *Personal Computing,* November 1978 (pp 69–70): fifteen listed specifications for microcomputers in various categories. Tables follow textual discussion. The aim was to pick the best microcomputers for teaching science students.

- *NCC Computer Hardware Record.* Three relevant issues: *Microcomputer Systems,* April 1978; *Microcomputer Development Systems,* March 1979; and *Small Business Computer Systems,* June 1979. Detailed information is given for micro devices and micro-based business systems (only UK- and Europe-available products included).

SELECTED MODELS

General

We describe below, in more detail, some important micro models and some less important ones. There is no attempt to give a profile of all the significant products on the market, or even of all the significant products from a key manufacturer (eg Intel, Motorola or Zilog). The aim is to give details of particular products to indicate the sort of devices available, developments in this particular field, and the international character of the microprocessor industry.

A year ago there were about twenty-five microprocessor architectures from about twenty manufacturers. In one list of 'all the available' architectures the author focuses on US companies (there is no mention of Ferranti or Toshiba). The manufacturers have enlarged their ranges (moving, for example, into increasingly sophisticated bit-slice architectures), and other manufacturers (in the US, Europe and Japan) have come to prominence since the following list was published (*Byte,* July 1978, p 124):

- Intel 8080, 8085, 8048, 8086;
- Motorola 6800;
- MOS Technology 6502;
- Zilog Z80, Z8000;
- Signetics 2650;
- RCA 1802;

- Fairchild F8, 9440;
- MOSTEK 3870;
- Intersil 6100;
- Texas Instruments 9900;
- National Semiconductor SC/MP, PACE, 8900;
- DEC LSI-11;
- Data General microNova;
- General Instrument 1600.

Today there is about twice this number of manufacturers supplying microprocessors to an ever-increasing range of 'second-source' producers. To the above list should now be added a wide range of microprocessor models from such companies as AEG Telefunken, American Microsystems, Essex International, Ferranti, NEC, Panasonic, Rockwell, Scientific Microsystems and Toshiba. In one comprehensive listing (*Electronic Design*, 11/10/78, p 62), no less than 148 microprocessor models from 41 manufacturers are listed, with 56 models being 'alternate source products' (ie there are now about one hundred microprocessor architectures being produced by primary manufacturers).

The extent to which particular models prevail depends in part upon the application area. For example, in personal computing four microprocessor models have been identified as 'the big four' – the Intel 8080, the Motorola 6800, the MOS Technology 6502 and the Zilog Z80. All these products, with a considerable amount of available software, are used in a wide range of applications (a profile of applications is given in Chapter 5).

Intel 8080

This microprocessor was the first of the second-generation 8-bit devices. It was announced in 1973 and has maintained an effective market lead since that time. An increasing number of competitors (eg the Motorola 6800) have attacked the Intel market share but the 8080 family still leads. The 8080 is used for personal computing, in dedicated industrial control applications, in stand-alone general-purpose minicomputers, and in a wide range of other applications.

There is more software available for the 8080 than for any other 8-bit device, and the microprocessor has good compatibility features (not just with the Intel 8085 and 8086 but with products from other manufacturers, eg the Z80). The 8080 is supplied by various companies including Intel, Advanced Micro Devices, National Semiconductor, Siemens, NEC and Texas Instruments. Well over half of all 8-bit microprocessors in use are 8080s. In the personal computing field alone various companies (eg Digital Group, E & L Instruments, Equinox, Heath Co, IMSAI, MITS, PolyMorphic, Processor Technology and Vector Graphic) are manufacturing systems based on the 8080.

Intel 8086

This device was intended to be compatible with the 8080 (or 8080A) but to possess, by virtue of the new 16-bit ALU width, vastly greater processing power. Additional processing capabilities not found in the original 8080 include 16-bit arithmetic, interruptible byte string operations, facilities for re-entrant code and dynamically relocatable programs. In some estimates the performance capability of the 8086 is equivalent to that of a minicomputer.

The 8086 microprocessor carries the equivalent of 29,000 transistors on the minute silicon chip. It comes with a family of additional components (called MCS-86), providing peripheral support, development software and design development aids.

The memory is a sequence of up to 1 million 8-bit bytes, compared with the 64K bytes of the 8080. Bytes can be paired to form 16-bit words. 64K addressable input or output ports are provided, as against the 256 I/O ports in the 8080. Ports may be 8- or 16-bit in size. The 8086 register set may be regarded as a 'superset' of the 8080 registers. The registers are used to provide a general register file, a pointer and index register file, a segment register file and a flag register file. (The purposes of the various files, and detailed system specification, are provided in the appropriate sources listed in the bibliography for Chapter 2.)

The instruction set includes most of the 8080 set, but has more power and flexibility. It can implement block-structured languages, with nearly all instructions operating on either 8- or 16-bit operands. There are four types of data transfer. The four arithmetic operations are available, with an additional logic instruction, *test*.

The 8086 was developed to meet the requirements of a broad range of new microprocessor applications. In time it may be expected to render the 8080 obsolete.

Intel 8022

The 8022 microcomputer is the first single-chip device to offer an analogue-to-digital converter. It has an 8-bit CPU, 64 bytes of random-access memory, a timer/event counter, etc — features of its 8021 predecessor. In addition there are various new and enlarged facilities. The read-only memory is 2 kilobytes and there are comparator inputs on eight input/output lines, five more digital I/O lines, full interrupt capability, and two 8-bit a-d input channels. The device was designed for ease of programming, many of the common routines being invisible to the user because they are carried out in on-chip hardware.

To perform an a-d conversion it is only necessary for the software to select the analogue input. The conversion is then carried out in hardware. In this way the program memory has scope for additional system functions. The instruction set can accommodate bit handling, binary and binary-coded decimal arithmetic, and there are facilities for input selection and input-based program jumps (*Electronics*, 20/7/78, pp 129–133).

Motorola 6801

This single-chip microcomputer combines nearly all the functions of the earlier seven-chip 6800. It carries CPU, random-access memory, read-only memory, timer and input/output requirements on the single chip, and is intended as a powerful, stand-alone controller. When added to one of the specialized 6800 peripherals, it can serve as a powerful, two-chip controller system.

The 6801 is a third-generation microcomputer system. It includes an improved 6800 CPU, 2 kilobytes of ROM, 128 bytes of RAM, three 16-bit timer functions, a serial I/O port, and 31 parallel, programmable I/O lines for peripheral control. The I/O lines are arranged in four ports, two of which bring out the chip's data bus and address bus. The buses are compatible with the 6800 bus system and can be directly attached to 6800 family peripheral and memory ports.

There is wide scope for multiprocessor applications. The 6801 architecture allows operation in various modes, each allowing the processors to communicate at a different speed and in ways appropriate to the configuration. For example, in a multiprocessor programmable peripheral controller the 6801 interconnects, as a peripheral device, to any CPU in the family (6800, 6802 or 6809) or to another 6801 bus.

Two 6801s may communicate, in the multiprocessor 'handshaking' mode, over the 8-bit bus from the third I/O port. Or, in the multiprocessor serial mode, several 6801s may communicate with each other over a single-wire serial I/O. Here one processor is the 'master' and the rest are 'slaves'.

The aim of the 6801, launched in 1978, was to reduce the cost of 6800 systems. In this context, compatibility with other 6800 devices was essential. 6800 programs will run on the 6801 which carries 10 new instructions in the set and also shortens the execution time of many conventional 6800 instructions. The 6801 has capability for six 16-bit operations. Other additional facilities include an 8-by-8-bit unsigned multiply that yields a 16-bit result in 10 microseconds, 20 times faster than the equivalent implementation in software in the 6800.

Motorola 6802/6846

This is a two-chip system intended to serve as a low-cost replacement for the 6800 in standard multichip designs. The 6802 microprocessor contains the 8-bit 6800 CPU. Together the two chips supply all the 6800 capability, plus 128 bytes of ROM for real-time scratch-pad operations, 2048 bytes of ROM for program storage, 10 parallel I/O lines for controlling peripherals and equipment linked to the system, and a 16-bit programmable timer.

The 6846 chip serves as combination ROM, I/O and timer. It contains 2 kilobytes of mask-programmable ROM, an 8-bit data port with control lines, and the programmable timer. The timer can be programmed in software. Interrupts can also be generated under software control.

Motorola 6809

This device extended 6800 capability into 16-bit applications. As with the 6801, it retains software compatibility. Users requiring certain 16-bit facilities, and already possessing 8-bit 6800s, do not need to move to a completely different product. 6800 capability is extended in the 6809 by the provision of extra registers, instructions, and addressing facilities. Internal buses have been expanded to 16-bits, and two 8-bit accumulators can be linked to form a 16-bit register for double-byte operations. The new 6809 circuitry has reduced the number of cycles required for the equivalent 6800 instructions.

The 6809 is the top-range device in the 6800 family. Processors can be chosen, from the one-chip 6801 through the two-chip 6802 and multi-chip 6800 to the 6809 microprocessor. There is hardware and software compatibility throughout. The 6809 provides high-level language-oriented facilities.

Zilog Z8

It is possible to distinguish between microprocessors that have evolved into single-chip microcomputers that emphasise input/output efficiency (often functioning as microcontrollers), and microprocessors that are memory-intensive machines (for number-crunching and data manipulation). Zilog developed an 8-bit single-chip architecture to serve both needs. The Z8 device may be regarded as either an I/O intensive microcomputer or as a memory-intensive microprocessor.

The Z8 can address external memory while maintaining as many I/O lines as possible. The address space can be expanded to 131,072 bytes while 15 I/O lines are retained. To allow the Z8 to serve its dual function, some spaces (such as external program memory and external data memory) have been separated, while others have been merged (such as I/O buffer storage and the register file).

The single Z8 chip carries: the CPU, running at an internal clock rate of 4 megahertz from an 8-MHz crystal; ROM (2048 bytes) for program storage; RAM (144 bytes) to constitute the register file; a receiver/transmitter; interrupts; and a pair of 8-bit timer-counters.

The 'handshaking' requirement, allowing communication between two identical processors, is well served by the Z8. This is seen as a particularly important provision in view of the increasing popularity of distributed systems. Complex communication is possible, either between identical Z8s or between a processor and its peripherals (*Electronics,* 31/8/78, p 131).

Zilog Z80

The 8-bit Z80 was introduced in 1976, and is available at a similar cost to the 6800. A large number of British microcomputer systems are based on the Z80. It is likely to remain the most popular microprocessor in the UK for domestic, educational and small business use.

The Z80 uses 16-bit addresses and can access up to 65,536 (64K) memory bytes. There is provision for RAM and ROM, used for data and program storage. Devices such as printers and keyboards can be connected to the Z80 buses, allowing them to respond to particular memory addresses. This technique of *memory-mapped* input/output is widely used in mini and microcomputers. There are also up to 256 input and 256 output ports for peripheral devices accessed under software control.

There is provision for 694 different instructions, variations of 158 basic types, broken down into eight major groups: load and exchange; arithmetic and logical; shift and rotate; jump, call and return; input/output; block transfer and search; bit manipulation; and general CPU control.

Zilog Z8000

This 16-bit device has helped to blur further the traditional distinctions between microcomputers and minicomputers. Zilog, aiming to make the Z8000 an industry standard, introduced it in 1978. It has been described as a monolithic minicomputer central processing unit with an instruction set more powerful than those in most minis. It is said to be faster than many minicomputers and two to five times faster than other 16-bit microcomputers. The Z8000 component family has applications in sophisticated data processing, high-speed communications, word processing, intelligent terminals and real-time process control.

Two versions of the Z8000 are available, partly to accommodate the trend towards larger memories: a 48-pin segmented version and a 40-pin unsegmented version. The 48-pin version is for use with an external memory-management device that allows variable segment sizes. Eight Mbytes of memory can be addressed. The 40-pin version addresses 64 kilobytes per address space.

The central processing unit includes sixteen 16-bit general-purpose registers, in addition to special system registers. The first eight of the 16-bit registers can be employed as 16 8-bit registers. Seven main data types are supported: bits, BCD digits, bytes, words (16 bytes), long words (32 bits), byte strings and word strings. The Z-bus system bus is essential to the Z8000 concept. It allows multiplexed address/data lines, 16-bit I/O addresses, and as much as 23-bit memory addressing using segmentation lines.

The Z8000 is based on NMOS technology and has a 4 MHz clock rate allowing cheaper dynamic RAMs. That the Z8000 can compete with minicomputers is highlighted by the fact that it is faster than the DEC PDP 11/45 and only a little slower than the PDP 11/70. Benchmarks have compared the Z8000 with the PDP 11/45 (*Microprocessors* and *Microsystems,* August 1978, pp 242–244).

(A possible microprocessor competitor to the Z8000 is the Motorola 68000, previewed at the September 1978 Wescon convention in Los Angeles. The 68000 contains 16 general-purpose 32-bit registers, a 24-bit program counter, a 16-bit condition code register, and a 16-bit ALU. All significant 6800/6801/6809 instructions have been included in the 68000 set. Six basic data types are supported: bits, 8-bit bytes, 16-bit words, 32-bit words, BCD digits and ASCII characters.)

National Semiconductor MM57109

This device is designed specifically for numeric processing, ie it is a 'number cruncher'. The instruction set has various sophisticated features such as floating decimal arithmetic, logarithmic and trigonometric functions. It can be used as a stand-alone device or to provide instrument intelligence. The 70 instructions are broken down into seven different classes: digit entry, data moves, math functions, clearing operations, branch functions, I/O, and mode control. The instructions are achieved with a 6-bit word. Scientific calculator operations are facilitated by the easy-to-use keyboard entry format.

Ferranti F100-L

The F100-L microprocessor was the first micro to be wholly designed and manufactured in Europe. It is a fast 16-bit, single-chip device, intended originally to compete with 16-bit products being manufactured in the US.

The project to develop and make the microprocessor was sponsored by the Ministry of Defence, and first examples of the F100-L were released for MOD projects in April 1976. There are now suggestions that the future of the device looks uncertain (*New Scientist,* 11/1/79, p 98). The Ministry of Defence may now declare a minicomputer standard based on a different architecture. One candidate is another Ferranti machine, the Argus M700. Technological developments which may facilitate a sophisticated Mark 2 version of the F100-L may also make it possible to put the M700 on a microprocessor chip. There are also doubts that the F100-L will have a worthwhile impact on the commercial market. Only about 5000 chips have been fabricated since inception of this architecture.

The F100-L was originally produced using the Ferranti CDI process. The production technique is claimed to allow for a high level of quality control. Typical instruction times are 3 to 4 microseconds. There are facilities for handling up to 32,000 16-bit words of fast semiconductor or core memory. Double-length operations are possible. A multiplexed I/O bus is employed and multiprocessor systems can be produced without the need for logic additions.

The origins of the F100-L meant that the focus was on military application. (One specification, for example, indicates that the device is capable of meeting the military operating temperature range of -55°C to $+125^{\circ}$C.) The original focus has tended to limit commercial development. There are no distributor support deals, discount pricing or second sourcing.

Toshiba T3444

The T3444, launched in August 1976, was Japan's first 8-bit microprocessor chip. Initial applications were in controllers for floppy disks, data cassettes and intelligent terminals. The 42-pin ceramic package carries a chip with an arithmetic/logic unit, RAM, ROM and input/output ports. The ROM can hold up to 256 24-bit words, with the RAM capacity being a modest 16 words by 8 bits. The instruction set is also modest, the 14 instructions being far fewer than in most 8-bit general-purpose micros. At the same time, the NMOS technology allows clock cycles as fast as 1.25 microseconds. Further, the equivalent of two instructions can be executed during one clock cycle.

To facilitate microprogramming and system debugging, there is a simulation board built out of 120 TTL packages, including two (Texas Instruments) 4-bit-slice ALUs. Socket provisions allow designers to try out alternative microprograms. Neither the chip nor the board carries a clock or I/O drivers. Designers are encouraged to try out particular clocks and drivers according to the required application.

Hewlett-Packard HP-67 and HP-97

These are 'personal computers' (programmable calculators). Both devices carry a full complement of mathematical functions and statistical functions. Other features include: Reverse Polish Notation; 26 data storage registers; register arithmetic; the capacity to record programs and data on magnetic cards; and an intelligent card reader. There is also an 'active pause' feature to allow the user to stop a running program and to display the answer for about one second. This facility also allows keyboard use and card insertion. The HP-67 and the 'older-brother' HP-97 are software-compatible.

Tutorial and Hobby Devices

A wide range of tutorial and hobby microprocessors are now available. The ones indicated here are typical (*Personal Computing,* November 1978, pp 60–70).

The *E & L MMD-1* is an expandable 8080-based system with data entered through an octal keypad and displayed in binary code. A Keyboard Executive Program is stored in a PROM (there is space for a second PROM).

The *IASIS-7301* is supplied in a ring binder with tutorial text, system service manual, programming card and programming scratch pad. Data is entered through a 24-key hex keypad and shown on eight 7-segment displays.

The *KIM-1* is accompanied by comprehensive manuals. Control is provided by a ROM program that monitors a keypad and controls a 6-digit display. Documentation includes the system user's manual, a hardware manual describing the implementation of the microprocessor and peripheral devices, and a programming manual.

The *Sol-20*, a terminal/computer system, can operate on a stand-alone basis or as an intelligent terminal. The system includes keyboard, power supply and main board. Either 8K or 16K of memory can be provided. There is comprehensive system documentation.

The *POLY-88* includes an expandable 5-slot S100 'motherboard', power supply, a cassette interface, 16K dynamic RAM, keyboard and video monitor. The system is completely operational without recourse to other hardware.

The *APPLE II* includes integer BASIC and Monitor in ROM (8K bytes), colour graphics, 4K RAM (exapandable to 48K), cassette interface, APPLE GAME I/O connector, ASCII keyboard, and power supply. *APPLE* was created in 1976 by two hobbyists working in a garage, (*Practical Computing,* July/August 1978, pp 12–13).

The *Altair 8800B* is the third generation of the most prolific hobby computer. The system includes power supply, 18-slot motherboard, CPU, front panel display and control circuitry. Boards are available in the S100 bus format. There is comprehensive supporting documentation.

The *VECTOR-1* includes power supply and an 18-slot motherboard. Apart from the power and reset buttons there is no provision of front panel control. An optional PROM/RAM board is available.

The *SWTP 6800* is based on the 6800 microprocessor. The system provides a low-cost alternative to the Altair S100 bus structure, and includes RAM (4K) and a TTY and RS232 interface.

The *SUPER JOLT* is a single-board microcomputer primarily intended for OEM use. It provides RAM (1024 bytes), 28 bi-directional I/O lines, interval timer, TTY and RS232 interfaces and a DEMON debug monitor. ROM (4K) can be purchased as an extra (contains tiny BASIC and a resident assembler program).

The *TI 990/100M* falls between a large microcomputer and a small minicomputer, and is built around the 16-bit TMS 9900 (with the same instruction set as Texas Instrument's 990 line of minicomputers). There are 256 words (expandable to 512 words) of RAM and an EPROM-based TIBUG monitor program.

The *Technico Super Starter Board (SSB),* another single-board microcomputer, is based on the TMS 9900 16-bit microprocessor from Texas Instruments. The system includes RAM (256 words expandable to 1K) and space for two 2708 PROMs. A monitor is provided on ROM.

The *Research Machine 380Z* is based on a Z80 CPU, with a monitor, VDU and keyboard. The VDU has a graphics capability as standard. Also included are an interactive text editor, 5K BASIC, 2K BASIC, utilities and games software. A flexible cable with sockets is used instead of a motherboard.

The *Tandy TRS-80* comprises four units: the keyboard-computer-VDU, a 12-in monitor, a power supply and a cassette deck. The system is based on a Z80 microprocessor. Level 1 BASIC is included in ROM. The VDU offers a graphics mode. Dynamic RAM (4K) is also provided.

The *PET* system is a popular home computer in the UK (1500 sold here and 3000 in the rest of Europe). It includes VDU, keyboard, cassette storage and other features. There are both RAM (8K expandable to 32K bytes) and ROM (13K bytes). A main attraction is the wide range of available software.

Intel 3000

The 3000 is a widely used bit-slice microprocessor. (It can be compared with other bit-slice systems from Fairchild, MMI,

TI, Mot and AMD.) It comprises a component kit which can be used to assemble a microcomputer or other digital machine quickly and flexibly. The system is intended for use in microprogrammed machines. Three basic components can be identified: the 3001 microsequence controller, the 3002 arithmetic unit (with registers), and the 3003 fast carry propagation unit.

The 3001 contains a microinstruction address register which can be connected directly to the address lines in microprogram ROM. Effective sequencing is determined by inputs from the current microinstruction and from the sequence control circuits. An important concept in the 3001 is the arrangement of the 512-word address space into 16 columns of 32 rows. The address-sequencing mechanism provides a number of different functions.

The 3002, 2-bit slice, contains the adder, 13 2-bit registers, multiplexers and buffers. The units can be used to build a complete arithmetic unit with any even number of bits per word. Where fast systems are required, the 3003 chip is used with up to eight 3002s comprising a carry lookahead unit. The 3002 has two distinct output buffers, three distinct data input buses, and provision for about 40 different functions to control the arithmetic logic and the multiplexers determining the inputs.

Documentation for the Intel 3000 assumes an understanding of bit-slice architecture.

Other Bit-Slice Systems

The 4-bit 6701 microprocessor device from Monolithic Memories, introduced in 1974, was the first bit-slice device. At that time it was marketed as a microcontroller rather than a microprocessor. In 1974 and 1975, Intel and Advanced Micro Devices introduced LSI circuits termed 'bipolar microprocessors'. Other companies – Fairchild, TI, Motorola, Raytheon, etc – quickly developed further bit-slice devices. There are currently six families of devices classified as bit-slice microprogrammable processor sets (listed in Chapter 1 under 'Bit-Sliced Architecture').

The 9405 (Fairchild) can be combined with the 9404 data-path switch to obtain a more powerful arithmetic processor contained in a space-economical 2-chip set. The 9405 is suitable for various controller and processor applications. Twice as many Intel 3002s as 9405s are required to implement a given-width processor. The 3002 works well in data manipulation tasks. A Signetics version, the N3002, is faster.

Various bit-slice systems, eg the Monolithic Memories 6701 and AMD's AM2901, are similar in architecture, featuring dual-port 16-register file and ALU cascading. These systems can cope with a wide range of applications. Various higher-speed versions of the 2901 are available from second sources. Texas Instruments has also launched several bit-slice architectures (eg the SBP0400, characterised by impressive programmable power dissipation). The MC10800 from Motorola, built with ECL, is the fastest bit-slice architecture and can be microprogrammed to perform multiply and divide. The most complex process element is the TI 74S481. The AM2903, a development of the 2901, is AMD's most recent bit-slice announcement.

PERIPHERALS

Specifications for microcomputers often give details of available peripherals. Systems are only effective if they can interact satis-factorily with users and the rest of the outside world. Peripherals may be named without full specification details. For example, the *NCC Computer Hardware Record* dealing with microcomputer systems states that available peripherals for the Ferranti F100-L are – paper tape reader, paper tape punch, keyboard, printer terminal, standard floppy disk drive, and magnetic tape cassette. Designers requiring detailed specifications will need to refer to manufacturers' literature or other sources.

Peripheral availability is often crucial to microcomputer effec-tiveness. For example, programmable I/O and peripheral devices, allowing the standardisation of hardware designs for system interfaces, have simplified the design of systems based on the single-chip 8080 microprocessor. The devices can be employed instead of the conventional logic assemblies using scores of digital circuits. The system designer's task focuses on organising external interface and interrupt structures. In the case of the 8080, typical key I/O and peripheral devices are the 8255 programmable peri-pheral interface (providing three ports for parallel I/O and control) and the 8253 programmable interval timer (consisting of three 16-bit BCD/binary counters).

Minicomputers can now be equipped with a wide variety of conventional computer devices, and microcomputers are rapidly catching up. Many peripheral manufacturers are producing buffered devices and interfaces that are easy to connect to microcomputers. Many new peripherals are from small suppliers that serve the personal and hobby computer markets, but the devices can be used more widely (for example, by OEMs that want to include them in systems).

Peripherals for microcomputers have to be smaller and lighter than those for minicomputers. For example, a DEC tape drive for the LSI-11 microcomputer measures 4 x 4 x 3 in. This device, the TU58, can store 512 blocks of data, each 512 bytes long. The identifiable trends are that peripherals are increasing in ability and reducing in price (*Electronic Design,* 11/10/78, pp 46–48). Peripherals and terminals can either link to microcomputers in the traditional architectural fashion or, to achieve intelligence, they can incorporate microprocessors as sub-units. In both these areas, systems are gaining in flexibility and power.

SOURCES OF FURTHER INFORMATION

The primary source of product information is the *manufacturers.* Sometimes it is useful to make a distinction between the *makers* of a device and other companies who may be able to *supply* it. As we have seen, the 8080 microprocessor, for example, can be supplied not only by Intel but by NEC, Siemens and other companies. Often a secondary supplier introduces enhancements or modifications, making available supporting documentation. Both manufacturers and suppliers are key sources of information.

Other sources are *research bodies* and similar organisations. Two important organisations in the UK carrying information on trends in the micro field are:

– Electrical Research Association,
  Cleeve Road, Leatherhead, Surrey, KT22 7SA

– The National Computing Centre,
  Oxford Road, Manchester, M1 7ED

Information can also be obtained from *books* and *journals.* In the rapidly moving field of microprocessor technology, books cannot hope to be completely up-to-date on product information. They are useful where they highlight historical trends or describe general and lasting principles of design and programming. Journals are usually more up-to-date: it is generally quicker to get an article in print than to publish a book. The journals cover the micro industry in detail from many angles – product development, system design, applications, programming, etc. It is worth listing the important journals devoted wholly or in substantial part to the various aspects of the microprocessor industry:

– *Microprocessors and Microsystems* (formerly *Microprocessors*)
  IPC Business Press Ltd, Oakfield House, Perrymount Road,
  Haywards Heath, Sussex RH16 3DH.

- *Mini-Micro Systems,* 270 St Paul Street, Denver, CO 80206
- *Byte,* Byte Publications Inc., 70 Main St., Peterborough NH 03458
- *Electronic Design,* Hayden Publishing Co Inc., c/o KLM Royal Dutch Airlines, SPL/KP, Shipol Airport, Amsterdam, Holland
- *Electronics,* McGraw-Hill Inc., 1221 Avenue of the Americas, New York NY 10020
- *Personal Computer World,* Intra Press, 62A Westbourne Grove, London W2
- *Personal Computing,* Benwill Publishing Corp., 1050 Commonwealth Ave., Boston MA 02215
- *Practical Computing,* Which Computer? 2 Duncan Terrace, London N1
- *Interface Age,* Mcpheters, Wolfe and Jones, 16704 Marquardt Ave., Cerritos, CA 90701

3 Software and Programming

INTRODUCTION

It used to be commonly said that microcomputers were weak on software. Hardware was seen as increasingly cheap and reliable, whereas the production of software was an expensive and time-consuming process. To some extent this situation is still true. At the same time microcomputers are approaching larger machines in programming scope and flexibility. An increasing range of programming languages and software packages is being made available at the micro end of the computer spectrum. It has been suggested that as microcomputers approach minicomputers in computing power and applications scope, it will be increasingly possible for micros to draw on the established reservoir of mini-computer software.

Microcomputer hardware is useless without programs to make it run. There are many different types of *programs* that comprise the *software* of the computer (some of these are described below). Some of the software may be machine-language programs under-stood directly by the computer. Other software may be high-level language programs that must be 'compiled' or 'interpreted' to machine language. Some software can help the user to develop specific applications programs, whereas other software (said to be 'canned' or 'packaged') comes ready to perform particular application functions.

Software considerations are crucial in selection of micropro-cessors and microcomputers. Ease of programming is essential to effective micro usage. Programs are sets of commands that tell the microprocessor how to perform. If it is difficult to organise the commands, or if they are limited in scope, the microcomputer will not be used effectively. Where the *instruction set* is straight-forward (see below) the device will be relatively easy to program and use. It is also important that there is an adequate range of

55

software available. If the microprocessor is in wide use then it is likely that many packaged programs will already be available. If a little-used microprocessor is chosen, the users themselves will have to develop the bulk of the required software. (It is often suggested in the literature that software considerations are more important in microprocessor selection than hardware factors such as speed and computing power.)

Emphasis is often given to the importance of sound software design. Adequate time devoted to this phase can save much trouble in the future; for example, during hardware and software debugging in system implementation. Software designers are encouraged to document their efforts, and to begin with input/output and diagnostic software. A straightforward diagnostic program can be used to pinpoint an integrated circuit (IC) breakdown where otherwise there may be a lengthy and fruitless search for a non-existent software bug. When the software is written it can be checked out in various ways — using a purpose-built development system, a cross-assembler and simulator, or the microcomputer configuration itself.

Many microcomputers make use of the BASIC high-level language (see below), suitable for many purposes (eg personal and hobby computing, business, industry, education and science). Increasingly, other languages are available. There has been some criticism of the development of machine-dependent software: the availability of 'universal programs' would clearly reduce the programming load on users. It is unlikely, however, that all applications needs will ever be satisfied by standardised software. Many users and design engineers will still have to learn how to program their microcomputers. The rest of this section gives a simple explanation of the fundamental programming terms and concepts.

Every *program* is built up out of a number of *instructions*. A group of instructions concerned with a particular task may be called a 'routine' or a 'sub-program'. For example, a data-processing program may comprise four separate routines, each a well-defined function written in isolation from the rest of the program. The individual instructions, routines and programs together make up the *software* of the machine. Microprocessor instructions stored in read-only memories (ROMs) are sometimes referred to as *firmware* to distinguish them from the 'hard' logic circuits and the 'soft' movable programs.

Instructions are represented in the microprocessor unit as unique sets of '1's and '0's. The various binary digits (bits) are decoded to cause the microprocessor to perform the necessary operations of logic, arithmetic, transfer, etc. The microprocessor decodes in *machine code,* ie handling the instructions in a representation that it understands. It is rare, however, for the programmer to represent any of the necessary instructions in the binary machine-code of '1's and '0's. The programmer usually writes the instructions in a suitable 'high-level' or 'source' language which the computer has to interpret, using other software, prior to processor decoding. *Source language* may be regarded as programming language understandable by the programmer but not by the microprocessor unit. An *assembler* is used to translate the source language into *object language* or *machine code* which the microprocessor unit can understand. (More details of the various software facilities and provisions are given under Software Development and Software Tools below.)

Programming microcomputers is similar to programming larger machines. However, there are fewer sophisticated aids available with micros. This can sometimes cause problems to mainframe program designers transferring to the micro scene (though not to engineers coming to software for the first time). Micro software still tends to be relatively primitive, small-scale and inflexible, but this is a rapidly changing situation.

INSTRUCTION SETS

Every microprocessor model has a unique *instruction set.* This set is the collection of instructions which the microprocessor is designed to understand and perform. In specification listings it is usual for details to be included about the instruction sets of microprocessors. For example, the number of instructions in a set will be given, and there may also be information about the instruction word size and the times taken to perform instructions of a certain type. Often specification details relating to a microprocessor are grouped with software information on available compilers, languages, debugging facilities, etc.

The size of the instruction set varies from one microprocessor to another. Some micros can cope with only a few dozen instructions, others with several hundred. It is sometimes convenient to group instructions into several classes of similar types within a set. In any event it is important that the user understands the instruction set in question: the available instructions, their scope and character, define the capabilities of the machine in various application contexts.

The number of instructions in a set is often used to make comparisons between different microprocessor models. The 16-bit TMS 9940E/9940M from Texas Instruments, for example, has 68 basic instructions in the set, whereas the Ferranti F100-L has 153. But care should be taken with such facile comparisons. It should not be assumed that a larger instruction set necessarily indicates a more versatile or more powerful device. For example, the same instruction can sometimes be applied in different ways (with different methods of addressing memory). An instruction set may be more flexible than a quick glance at the number of available commands suggests. Or a large instruction set may truly indicate a powerful device. It is important to take into account all the relevant considerations.

Instruction sets are often quoted in terms of the number of executable source program commands, each of which may assemble into one or more bytes of machine code. The M6800 microprocessor from Motorola, for example, has 72 source-language instructions, forming 197 valid machine codes upon assembly. In operation, instructions are normally held in ROM. The memory is addressed sequentially, causing instructions to be fed into the microprocessor one at a time for decoding. Following decoding, the instruction is obeyed.

The instruction sets for particular microprocessor models generally include the basic arithmetic operations (add, subtract, etc) and the basic logic operations (AND, OR, etc). Some sets do not include logic functions, and in other devices subtraction and other operations may have to be carried out by means of a cumbersome multi-instruction sequence. Many sophisticated commands common in mainframe instruction sets are absent in microcomputers. Increasingly, however, there is provision for such facilities as floating point arithmetic. The most sophisticated instruction sets include facilities for arithmetic, logic, transfers, I/O control, conditional jumps, etc. (For example, the instruction set for the Texas Instruments TMS-9900/SBP-9900A microprocessor models resembles that for many minicomputers. The 69 commands provide 26 arithmetic, logic and data manipulation instructions, 14 internal register-to-memory operations, five data transfer commands, and 24 control functions. The instructions include facilities for binary multiply and divide, as well as provisions for 16 prioritized interrupts, and programmed and DMA I/O capability.)

The instruction word size is often defined in specification listings. For example, the word size for the General Instrument

CP1600 is given as 10 bits. This microprocessor is a 16-bit device, ie the data word is comprised of 16 bits. The most rapidly performed instruction in the CP1600 set, a command in the control group, takes 1.6 μS; the longest instruction, in the jump group, takes 4.8 μS. In The Texas Instruments TMS-9900 microprocessor, for example, the shortest instruction (branch) takes 2 uS. and the longest (divide) takes 32 μS. In general there is a relationship between the instruction word size and the data word size. It is often required that operands (ie the quantities participating in computation) and instructions are held in the same memory. For this reason the instruction length is conventionally equal to the data word length or is a multiple of it.

The size of the instruction word determines the amount and complexity of information that can be processed when a single command is obeyed. The bits of the instruction word variously specify addresses of operands and the particular order (add, OR, transfer, etc) to be performed. In some instances, an order of a particular type may cause the nominal address bits in the instruction word to be interpreted as an operand, not as the *location* of an operand. This facility, typical in mainframe computers, may be absent in some microprocessor systems.

Programmed instructions are usually obeyed sequentially. A running program counter updates the instruction address progressively, allowing orders to be performed one after another. Each instruction, containing operand and command information, is extracted from store, then decoded and obeyed. Decoding allows specified operands to be identified and subjected to decoded commands. However, the sequential execution of program can be delayed or interrupted in various circumstances. Jump orders, for example, can take over from the program counter and specify the next instruction. Where the appropriate order is specified in the instruction word, other parts of the word define the address of the next instruction to be obeyed.

Jump instructions may be *unconditional* or *conditional.* They may cause a non-sequential jump in program *whenever* they are decoded, or *only* when some other condition is satisfied (eg when the contents of a register specified in the instruction word are greater than a particular value). The specific jump order itself, specified by the appropriate bits in the instruction word, may have this conditioned or unconditioned character; or the order may be 'ambiguous', relying for precision on the state of 'flag' bits elsewhere in the instruction word.

Instructions allowing a non-sequential jump in the order of command execution are often referred to as *program control* instructions. They do not in themselves specify operations such as subtraction or masking. Program control instructions are hence distinguished from the *operation* instructions that form the major part of the instruction set.

A main purpose of jump instructions is to allow entry to a routine held at a specific place in a program. This type of jump is often called a 'subroutine call'. The call indicates that the next instruction address to be effective will be the address of the first instruction in the routine. The various operation instructions in the routine are obeyed, after which a return is made to the original point in the main program from which the call was made. Therefore at the time a call is actioned, it is necessary for the system to remember the address of the call instruction. This allows a return to be made to the main program when the routine (or 'subprogram') has been performed.

Jump orders, together with operation orders and other facilities, help to define the flexibility and scope of the instruction set. The character of the instruction set, in turn, defines the power of the microcomputer in question.

THE LANGUAGE SCENE

An increasing range of programming languages is available for use with microprocessors. Some of these languages are variants of systems used with mainframes and minicomputers. Others are languages specifically designed for use in the microprocessor context. The languages vary according to their degree of machine dependence, their general scope, and the tasks for which they are best suited.

The 'level' of a language is recognised by how closely its statements mirror or model the individual processor operations. A low-level language is one where individual statements tightly model machine operations. Assembly language is generally regarded as typical low-level language, the most direct way of programming a computer.

Ideally, the program code for a processor would be set out in the '1's and '0's that the circuitry could understand and obey without time-consuming interpretation. The writing of such 'absolute' code is not easy for the programmer: it is difficult to write out and understand, and mistakes are likely. Assembly code is one stage removed from binary code. Typically, mnemonics are decoded (or 'assembled') into absolute machine-readable code. As an example, an instruction in the Intel 8080 microprocessor to move the contents of Register L into Register E is keyed in at a terminal as

MOV E, L

After the assembly stage this becomes the 8-bit binary instruction, 01011101.

Use of assemblers represents a direct programming method, allowing effective control over microprocessor architecture and fast execution times. They can be seen, with compilers, as an intermediate stage, used to translate higher-level source programs into machine code. They can also be used to print a program listing that displays together the source and object versions of the program, providing at the same time error and other useful diagnostic information.

The high-level languages have algorithmic statements rather than ones that are machine-oriented. These languages make for easier programming but are more removed from machine code. They save time in the development phase and are generally used where software is intended for operation on a small number of processors. Conversely, with large production quantities, use of assembler can yield significant memory savings. Selecting a high-level language depends upon the particular application. It also depends upon the availability of assemblers and compilers for the microprocessor in question.

In high-level *application* languages, the primitive operations handle arithmetic tasks, character strings and I/O functions. These languages, suitable for problem-solving in science and business, have been widely accepted in the mainframe environment. An increasing range of microprocessor system problems is being tackled using the available high-level application languages.

High-level *system* languages, characterised by algebraic notation and high-level control structures for such tasks as process scheduling and resource management, are particularly relevant to current microprocessor operations. A systems language used with microprocessors should be well defined in syntax and semantics, and should be competent in computing resource management (eg register and memory supervision). It is also necessary that the language allows full access to the processor architecture. A danger of high-level language forms is that access to the full operational capability of a microprocessor is sometimes obscured, a problem less evident in the mainframe systems. The operations normally available via assembly language must be accessible. The PLZ family of languages has been represented as an attempt to meet language objectives in the context of microcomputer system software development (*Computer*, March 1978, pp 34–39).

The programmer using high-level language needs fewer lines of code than in assembler to make a system operate. Such languages make heavy demands on memory, a limiting factor for small-memory microcomputers. Up to a dozen machine instructions can be produced from one high-level language statement, a circumstance that allows high-level usage to decrease the effective coding time.

High-level languages allow the programmer to concentrate on the problem to be solved. There is no immediate concern with processor idiosyncracies, with the contents of this or that register or memory location. The programmer can set out the instructions in 'friendly' symbols that resemble conventional English usage: IF, THEN, ELSE, REPEAT, DO, JUMP, etc. There is less need for accompanying comment on the program chart, and the flow diagram phase of development may be eliminated altogether.

Since high-level languages are less machine-dependent than assembly languages, high-level code is more *generally* useful than assembly code. High-level code is more portable, more easily transferred from one system to another.

It is convenient to develop firmware using a high-level language. Routines are relatively short, portable and near in appearance to conventional English. Particular high-level instructions rarely compile into machine code instructions on a one-to-one basis. This is because the contents of various hardware stores have to be cleared or modified before meaningful assembly-language instructions are generated. The programmer, operating in high-level language, is indifferent to internal machine activity, except insofar as a proliferation of machine-code steps may affect the duration of routines.

The relative portability of high-level languages has led to speculation about the possibility of a standard high-level language for microcomputers. A universal language would reduce the user's current dependence on a particular hardware supplier and would help to control escalating software development costs. Such a language would have to be general-purpose and self-documenting. It would also exhibit flexible data handling and input-output capacities. PASCAL (see below) is thought by many to be the most likely candidate.

It is difficult to compare individual high-level languages for performance except in tight and excessively artificial circumstances. Constraints of modularity and structure, often unanticipated, can affect a programmer's activity. Benchmark routines normally assume that the programmer uses the full power of the language without knowledge of the type of code it produces. In fact, much more efficient code can be produced if the programmer is well aware of what the language can do well and what it does poorly. In one estimate (*Electronics*, 3/8/78, p 118), an efficiency increase of 30% can be achieved within two weeks if time is spent learning the characteristics of the language.

There are hundreds of available high-level languages for systems and applications purposes. Increasingly these are bearing on the microcomputer scene. With the rapidly diminishing cost of computer memory, the advantages of high-level languages are increasingly available to micro users. Sometimes available languages are unsuitable for a particular application and it is necessary to design a new language: a recent example is WEMAP from Westinghouse (*Mini-Micro Systems,* October 1978, pp 90, 92–93). Some of the principal languages of importance to microprocessor users are profiled below.

SOME AVAILABLE LANGUAGES

PL/M

Most early high-level languages for microprocessors derived from IBM's general-purpose PL/1. The Intel version for both systems and applications programming on the 8080 is termed PL/M (*Electronics,* 27/6/74, p 103). The PL/M compiler is a Fortran IV program, suitable for use on any 32-bit host processor. Many PL/M compilers are available to run on 16-bit minicomputers. PL/M was created to help designers working with the 8008 chip. Now a much enhanced version is available for use on the 8086.

Following the early widespread usage of PL/M (eg by Sycor, the Michigan-based manufacturer of intelligent terminals), a range of PL/M-type high-level language compilers quickly developed: SMPL (for National Semiconductor IMP-16 devices), PL/M 6800 and PL/W (both for the 6800), PL μS (for the Signetics 2650), and PL/Z (for the Zilog Z80 − see below).

MPL

MPL is generally represented as one of the small number of early specially tailored high-level microprogramming language systems (AFIPS, SJCC, 1971, pp 169–177). Others are SIMPL (IEEE *Transactions on Computers,* C-23, August 1974) and PUMPKIN (*SIGMICRO Newsletter,* 5, 1974, pp 45–76). An increasing range of tailored languages is now available.

The language MPL, like PL/M, derives from PL/1. It was originally implemented for the Interdata 3 microprocessor, and is structured in the same way as PL/1. The translation sequence from MPL source programs to absolute binary microcode comprises four phases. The first phase involves conversion into an intermediate language called SML, used in the second phase to generate virtual symbolic object microcode. Phase 3 uses a created dictionary to carry out further conversions. In the final phase the symbolic object code is assembled by the Interdata 3 microcode assembler. A SNOBOL4 program is used to convert SML to Interdata 3 microcode.

SIMPL

An aim of SIMPL, derived from ALGOL, is to detect operations which may be carried out in parallel and to optimise microcode in various ways. The language can aid efficiency by minimising the number of registers employed in the internal microprocessor architecture. A SIMPL compiler is available for the Tucker/Flynn microprocessor, first developed nearly a decade ago. The compilation procedure is seen as largely machine-independent, but the data required in the initial phases has machine-dependent features. It is recognised that early SIMPL has some awkward coding features and is unsuitable for code generation in many microprocessors. To overcome the various limitations an effective family has been evolved (V. R. Basili, *The SIMPL Family of Programming Languages and Compilers,* Department of Computer Science, University of Maryland, 1976).

PUMPKIN

This language is based on the systems implementation language called LSD, itself an early derivation of PL/1. PUMPKIN was designed for the microprogrammed control unit of a signal processing element, a machine developed by the US Navy. The PUMPKIN compiler retains many MPL features, and there are other similarities between the two languages. PUMPKIN (*SIGMICRO Newsletter,* 5, 1974, pp 45–76), as with the other early tailored languages, have had to face mounting competition from newer systems.

PLZ

Zilog's PLZ, implemented in a set of disk-based programs that run under the RIO (relocatable input/output) operating system, is in effect a family of languages intended to serve the microcomputer environment. Each of the PLZ languages has identical features which can be expanded to form the different systems in the family. The various languages can be applied in the areas where they are best suited, to be linked together at a later stage into a single program. PLZ has the flexibility to allow a combination of high-level, machine-independent modules with low-level machine-dependent modules in the same program. The PLZ/SYS language, used by the high-level modules, blends elements of PASCAL, ALGOL, PL/1 and C to facilitate expression of algorithms in a high-level structured fashion.

PLZ is procedure-oriented and intended to provide easy-to-learn languages. Selection of PLZ/ASM, which includes assembly instructions, allow direct access to the machine architecture. The translation process is relatively straightforward because of the character of the central grammar common to all the languages in the family. The grammar contains high-level statements that can be converted easily into efficient machine-language sequences. PLZ/ASM, with its direct access to microprocessor capability, is a low-level system programming language. Similar to PL/360, it is constructed by adding assembly language features to the central PLZ kernel. The assembly language is that of the Z80 microprocessor. High-level data declarations can be combined with low-level instructions: there is access to low-level processes without the need to reduce all programming tasks to low-level machine dependency.

PLZ/SYS, as a high-level language, has no direct access to microprocessor architecture. A task can be partitioned into PLZ/ASM and PLZ/SYS modules according to the levels of the various requirements. The modules can be linked into a single program once they have been translated into machine code. Other PLZ languages for specific purposes are being contemplated (eg for co-ordinating concurrent processes, for text processing, and for graphics). There is evident worth in the language-family concept: a common kernel can allow expansion into a range of mutually compatible languages for different purposes.

COBOL

The popularity of COBOL in the mainframe and minicomputer environments is reflected in commercial programming for microprocessors. There is clearly a vast market for microprocessor-based business systems using COBOL.

MicroFocus, a small software house and microprocessor consultancy, produced the first COBOL compiler for microprocessors. They have produced a resident compiler for the Z80 and for the 8080/8085, which at the end of 1978 was selling for around £400. To a subset of ANS 74 standard were added extensions to aid interactive working, program control of files, file handling and rapid development. There have been various sales made in Europe: for example, to Tandberg (for their desktop terminals) and to the French microcomputer firm R21 (for their Micral range of systems). MicroFocus are offering the software for sale on Intel's Series II development system as part of a turnkey package. Further enhancements to the compiler are envisaged.

Microsoft (USA) have also developed a COBOL compiler for the 8080/8085 and Z80 (priced at $750 in late-1978). Again it uses ANS 74 standard features plus various additional facilities. Motorola have developed a 24K byte resident compiler for the 6800 microprocessor, written basically for use on the Exorcizer Development Series. Data General run COBOL on the MicroNova 16-bit computer cards, though the compiler facilities are only available on the CS20 terminal.

The British firm CAP MicroSoft has evolved a host software development MicroAde, under which MicroCOBOL can be used. The method can allow programs to be crosstranslated to run on different machines. 'Commercial code' is produced for interpretation by the specific hardware. Some application packages are available (eg sales ledger, time recording, Autoclerk, purchase ledger, etc), and MicroCOBOL programs can be generated within the MicroAde context. MicroAde facilitates software development for 8080/8085, 6800, Z80 and other microprocessors.

NRDC (UK) is funding MicroCOBOL development by CAP, with additional backing for implementation and marketing. The National Computing Centre is supporting development of accounting applications. MicroAde/MicroCOBOL has been bought by various UK organisations, including the Central Computer Agency, Newcastle University and Prudential Assurance.

Zilog have made resident COBOL available for the MCZ−1

range of microcomputers. The compiler is based on ANS 74, Level 1, with enhancements and some Level 2 features. In early-1978 the new COBOL facility was claimed by Zilog to be "a major step in the utilisation of the powerful features of the Z80A for general-purpose business computing."

FORTRAN

FORTRAN, like COBOL, has been adapted from traditional computer practice, to meet various microcomputer requirements. It is available on an increasing range of microprocessor-based systems. For example, Digital Equipment supplies FORTRAN software (with BASIC and CORAL) for the LSI-11/PDP-11/03; Data General supplies FORTRAN software for the MicroNova series; General Automation for the GA-16/110; Comart for the Z-2.

Various versions of FORTRAN can be made available for the same basic microprocessor. FORTRAN in three versions can be supplied for the Intel 8080:

— Intel's own version, FORTRAN 80;

— a version from Microsoft (USA);

— a version from Realistic Controls (USA), this being a FORTRAN dialect lacking some facilities.

Some micros are descended from minicomputers, a circumstance that favours utilisation of existing software. This applies with various 16-bit micros, eg DEC's LSI 11 and Data General's MicroNova (both mentioned above) and TI's 9900 systems. A relatively new FORTRAN compiler from Zilog, for the Z80, runs under RIO in 48K bytes and cost £644 (late-1978).

MicroFORTH

This language was originally developed for minicomputer control applications. Problems are defined by means of an application-oriented vocabulary of commands compiled into machine code and stored on floppy disk. The stored dictionary occupies the bulk of program memory and defines the terms in the vocabulary. MicroFORTH finds words in the dictionary, adds words, and recognises contexts that select parts of the dictionary.

MicroFORTH, free from syntax, is easy to test. Efficient use is made of memory and it can be more compact, for programs over 2K, than machine code programs. There are however some execution time problems. The language is available for various development systems, including Intel's MDS, Motorola's Exorcizer and Zilog's UDS. MicroFORTH is supplied on floppy disk with manuals and program listings.

CORAL

CORAL 66, based on ALGOL 60, was developed at the Royal Signals and Radar Establishment, Malvern, UK. Early in 1978, Britain's home-grown Ferranti F100-L microprocessor was made available with a Coral 66 compiler developed by Systems Designers Ltd. The aim was to satisfy the need for an efficient high-level language for real-time microprocessor systems. At about the same time as the F100-L announcement, SDL's Coral 66 compiler was released for the Texas Instruments 9900/990 range.

GEC Semiconductors have developed a resident CORAL 66 compiler, the RCC 80, for the 8080 microprocessor. The 8-bit facility includes the full range of standard operators and some additional ones. Dual floppy disks are recommended. The IECCA (Inter Establishment Committee on Computer Applications) has approved the GEC compiler, and more than 40 users have taken licences. GEC are considering implementing CORAL 66 on the 8086 microprocessor.

PASCAL

There is a growing trend towards the use of PASCAL. It has proved very popular as a hobbyist language and is gaining ground among engineering/computer graduates. It has the qualities of clarity and ease-of-use, and encourages the formulation of thinking in a structured way. PASCAL is represented as a very powerful tool for writing interactive business application programs on both microcomputers and minicomputers. It provides data structuring facilities superior to those of COBOL, and its control constructs encourage a systematic and modular approach to program design (reducing development effort and improving reliability).

Principal users of PASCAL are the University of California, San Diego (UCSD) and the US Stanford Linear Accelerator Group. Both these users have produced compilers for the Z80. UCSD PASCAL is fully interactive in the small computer environment, yet offers many features normally found only on medium- and large-scale computers. It will operate on most microcomputers or minicomputers based on 8-bit bytes or 16-bit words. Versions are available for such microprocessors as the LSI-11, the 8080 and the Z80. PASCAL was first made available to users in August 1977 and is now in use on dozens of mainframes using these and other processors.

The machine-independent character of PASCAL has naturally led to speculation about its possible emergence as a high-level operating system. PASCAL is, for example, effective in distributed processing, and software can even be transported from micro to mainframe without need for changes in the internal source code. (Fortran, by contrast, requires major modification to the assembly-level code when switched to a different system). At the same time there are reservations about PASCAL, but TI have announced that all internal programming is performed in PASCAL. Intel aims to develop a PASCAL compiler but not an operating system. Companies currently committing resources to PASCAL include American Microsystems, Western Digital Corporation and General Automation. (The interest in PASCAL is reflected in the literature. See bibliography and in particular *Byte,* August 1978.)

BASIC

BASIC (Beginner's All-purpose Symbolic Instruction Code) was designed in 1964 at Dartmouth College in the US. It was intended, as its name implies, to be a very simple, easy-to-use language from which students and other users would progress to the more power-ful high-level languages such as FORTRAN, COBOL, ALGOL and PL/1. The grammatical rules of BASIC are simple and it resembles straightforward English more than does any other high-level language. Use is made of words such as IF, THEN, GOTO, STOP and NAME.

Though simple to understand, BASIC is still a powerful high-level language, suitable for use in a wide range of mathematical and business situations. The simple nature of BASIC means that interpreters and compilers for the language are small, rendering BASIC very suitable for microprocessor-based systems where storage may be limited. Recognition that BASIC is not suitable in some applications (eg in some areas of teaching) has led to con-sideration of other language possibilities (such as PILOT – see below). At the same time, BASIC continues to be used very widely in the microprocessor environment.

Now BASIC has many dialects. Put another way, there are many different BASICs. The American National Standards Insti-tute has approved a Minimal BASIC. There are in fact many expansions, modifications and additions to the original Dartmouth

BASIC, and available compiling BASICs are very distinctive. Two compilers for the M6800, one from Microwave Systems Corporation and the other from Software Dynamics, have been compared (*Practical Computing*, July/August 1978, pp 24–25).

BASIC can provide file handling, fast execution, good arithmetic capabilities and impressive portability (though the dialect scene complicates transferability). BASICs have been classed as either interpretive or compiling, almost all being interpretive (and conversational). Where a BASIC can allow a machine to compile a program into machine code, programs will typically be executed several hundred times faster than where the compiler facility is absent. Benchmarks have been used to show that properties of BASICs vary considerably.

PILOT

PILOT (sometimes called CORE PILOT or PILOT 73) was originally devised at the San Francisco Medical Centre. Like BASIC, PILOT was intended to be easy to understand and use, particularly suitable for the teaching environment. COMMON PILOT is a refinement of the original concept. Several versions of PILOT have been described in the microcomputer journals. It is seen basically as a computer-aided instruction (CAI) language, designed and implemented by experienced CAI authors. Again, as with BASIC, the inevitable dialect situation has developed. Systems have been developed for the 6800 microprocessor and for other microprocessor systems.

SOFTWARE TOOLS

It is worthwhile – partly to summarise and partly to introduce new terms – to survey the range of available *software tools* or *support software*. The software tools and aids available for a particular microprocessor bear directly on ease of program development for the system, and on system costs and capabilities. With microprocessors, software costs are proportionately high since hardware costs are low.

Assemblers (and *compilers*) are programs that translate source programs to object programs, the actual array of binary digits interpreted by the processor. In assembly language there is normally a small ratio between statements in the language and instructions in object (or machine) code. Assemblers are sometimes termed *translators*, ie they translate assembly code to machine code.

Simulators are used on a larger computer to test the object program by simulating the action of the microcomputer. The processes of software testing and debugging can be speeded up because of the superior capabilities of the larger machine. Features can be added to the simulator which would be outside the scope of the microprocessor. For example, the simulator can incorporate explicit error messages, traps for illegal conditions, and diagnostics, for attempts to write into read-only memory. Simulators cannot wholly replace program testing on the microprocessor itself.

Debuggers facilitate testing of the object program on the microcomputer. They accept commands from the user to carry out such operations as displaying or printing out the contents of the microcomputer memories or registers, modifying RAM, running the object program from a specific point, and stopping the program as required. The activities of debuggers are supplemented by those of simulators.

Editors convey the source program, written in assembly or high-level language and entered through a keyboard or paper tape, into a file on disk or tape. The editor program acts on commands from the user to add or delete parts of the source program in the auxiliary tape or disk memory. Editors vary in scope: some only operate on entire lines in a program, whereas others can manipulate specific character strings.

Loaders transfer the object program from an external medium (eg paper tape) to random-access memory in the microcomputer. Some loader programs convert a relocatable version of the object program to a loadable form. Where a program's initial address has been changed by compiler action, a loader can be used to modify all addresses accordingly in the object program.

SOFTWARE DEVELOPMENT

Effective software development presupposes available software tools and a suitable language (usually high-level). A system implementation language such as PASCAL helps to optimize hardware use. An applications language such as FORTRAN facilitates statement of the problem.

A choice can also be made between *resident* and *cross development* systems. A resident facility produces object code to run on its own processor, whereas a cross-software system executes on one processor and generates results as if it were executing on another. For example, a cross-assembler for an 8080 microprocessor could run on a large computer but translate the same assembly language into the same 8080 machine language as would an 8080 resident assembler. Cross development systems are generally much faster than simple resident systems. An example development sequence (*Electronic Design,* 19/7/78, p 65) gives a typical total job time as 109 hours for resident development and just over 13 hours for cross development.

Software development may be regarded as proceeding according to identifiable phases. In one breakdown (*Computer,* June 1978, p 37), development time is distributed over definition and design (30 per cent), writing program code (20 per cent), and system integration and testing (50 per cent). It is notoriously true that allocated times for software development are often overrun, often because little or no time has been given to testing. Project managers are advised to establish intermediate project milestones.

In addition to the specific types of software used in development (profiled above), there are other classes of hardware- and hardware/software-based development aids. *PROM programmers,* facilitating program loading into PROM, are essential for debugging requirements, particularly important in the final stages of product development. *Oscilloscopes* may be regarded as a primitive debugging aid, as are *programmer panels* (displays resembling the computer front panel).

Microprocessor prototyping kits aid learning about microprocessors but have limited use as a development aid. *Logic* and *microprocessor analyzers* extend the facilities of the simple oscilloscope and can aid programmer productivity, and use can also be made of *emulators* and specific *paper-tape-based microprocessor development systems.* Development systems, microcomputers themselves, are equipped with monitors, text editors, language translators (assemblers and compilers), and debugging programs. Low-speed paper-tape peripherals can represent a major limitation. Sophisticated development aids may include *larger computer systems, disk-based microprocessor development facilities,* and *in-circuit emulators.*

The sophisticated aids cover all phases of the development process, eg document writing, program development and testing. Peripheral performance may be a limiting factor in project execution. Aids, of whatever type, can be purchased or rented.

AVAILABLE PACKAGES

As with mainframes and minis, there is a growing range of off-the-shelf software packages available for microcomputers. These are produced by the hardware manufacturers or by independent software houses. For example, the UK firm Petsoft specialises in writing and selling software for the Commodore Pet microprocessor, popular in the personal computer field. Petsoft has issued a catalogue featuring more than 100 business, educational and applications programs. A mortgage package is available for £7 (late-1978), a life-expectancy package (£5), etc. And mathematical packages are available for operations with prime factors, quadratics, combinations and permutations, and other functions.

One problem with software packages is that, with a rapidly changing hardware scene, new architectures tend to outflank off-the-shelf software products. As in the large computer environment, there is the perennial debate about whether to program from scratch for a given application or to seek out (and modify if necessary) a pre-existing software product. Users can only be advised to find out − from manufacturers, suppliers, and software houses − what software is available for particular microcomputers and to judge how well particular requirements are met.

STRUCTURED PROGRAMMING

The increasing focus on microprocessor programming and software, in circumstances of rapidly diminishing hardware costs, has led to consideration of methods of improving program generation and reliability. *Structured programming* aims to reduce the programming task to manageable steps, making programs easier to write and easier to understand.

Use is made of a limited set of well-defined control structures. The indiscriminate use of branches (GOTO statements) is avoided: the aim is to make program execution continue in a forward direction except for controlled program loops. The various program steps are independently arranged, allowing effective checking at each stage. Errors can be systematically detected, and the overall structure allows rigorous proof of the correctness of the entire algorithm.

Structured programming is related to *modular programming* and the implementation of *top-down* techniques. The structural character of a program can be enhanced by dividing it into functional modules. Each module should ideally carry out a single function or a group of related functions. One rough guideline is that a module should not exceed 50 program statements. The *top-down* approach lays emphasis on the overall program design, moving cautiously and without excessive modularisation, to smaller functional areas.

Problems in microprocessor programming demand aids to efficient organisation and structuring of software. The growing relevance of structured programming and related techniques to microprocessor applications is reflected in the literature (see bibliography).

It is also important to realise that whereas much traditional programming practice is relevant to the micro scene, there are a number of areas – handling of interrupts, control of peripherals, optimum use of memory, etc – where an approach uniquely appropriate to microprocessors is required. One example may be given – the handling of multilevel subroutines and interrupts in microcomputers (*Computer Design,* January 1978, pp 109–115).

SOFTWARE PERFORMANCE

It is important to know the limitations of system software. Only then can the best use be made of the microprocessor, the memory facilities and I/O provisions. System performance can be monitored to provide information on limiting factors, whereupon efforts can be made to improve inefficient routines. One way of collecting the necessary information is to sample the address bus periodically: a map of memory addresses can be produced with their corresponding frequency of reference.

Microprocessor memory usually stores both program and data. Address samples in program storage can correlate processor activity with specific program segments. Software bottlenecks can be identified by this means.

The samples can be used to identify program segments that are operating inefficiently. System monitors can provide information on memory and bus usage, thus facilitating the optimization of program segments. A detailed description of a system monitor comprising an M6800 microprocessor, a ROM or PROM for program storage and a RAM for scratchpad storage and data accumulation is available (*Electronic Design,* 7/6/78, pp 122–126).

Sometimes it is necessary to arrange tradeoffs between hardware and software elements in order to maximise efficiency in particular application circumstances. The amount of hardware can be reduced by making the software more complex, and conversely additional hardware can reduce software requirements. In some cases it is relatively straightforward to decide on necessary hardware provisions whereas software elements are harder to provide. Data-acquisition systems, for example, based on modular hardware, often require flexible software, able to cope with rapidly changing circumstances. In a typical application the aim may be to provide a structured software arrangement, allowing both standard routines and others that are easy to modify or replace.

The scope for efficient software performance is a key factor in opting for a particular microprocessor system. It is a central interest of the designer aiming to achieve effective applications for minimum cost.

4   Thinking about Design

INTRODUCTION

There are many 'levels' of design. Designers may focus on individual components (memories, buses, arithmetic-logic units, clocks, etc), on microcomputers (built up out of selected components), or on larger systems in which a microcomputer (or a microcomputer array) is regarded as a single component. The level of design determines the areas and considerations relevant to the designer's activities. Someone designing a new RAM or ROM will be interested in the physics of semiconductor materials. A designer of microcomputers, using available elements, will be more interested in component compatibility, timing characteristics, reliability and other performance features. And design of larger systems in which microcomputers are components implies an awareness of both computing and non-computing engineering constraints. Any general discussion of design, such as the present chapter, presupposes that design can occur at different levels and that these determine the interest of the designer.

THE IMPACT OF MICROPROCESSORS

Microprocessor-based systems are influencing the market scene in many ways. For example, they are increasingly being considered as alternatives to minicomputers. They are also being used to replace certain types of pre-existing circuitry (hardwired logic). Where microprocessors are used to replace ordinary TTL circuits, an element of design flexibility is created. The designer can make preproduction changes, adding new features at the prototype stage without having to lay out new circuit boards or to increase the number of components. Later changes to units in operation are relatively easy to incorporate in microprocessor-based systems.

Part of the impact of the microprocessor is due to its 'universally usable' characteristic. The microprocessor may be regarded as a general logic circuit which performs the specific functions

77

defined by the program. In some instances – as with clocks, calculators and controllers – the microprocessor is the major part of the machine hardware.

The superiority of microprocessors to TTL equivalents is shown in terminal design. Microprocessors cope much more easily with functions such as programmable carriage control, data rate buffering, and variable communications codes and character sets. Microprocessor software developments are spread over quantity sales. Where microprocessors are used to replace other computers, software considerations are of particular importance. A designer may demand a microcomputer for a specific application requiring small hardware size, portability and low power consumption. At the same time the designer may have to tolerate high software costs.

In considering a computer – micro, mini or mainframe – for a particular application, the designer has to look at the tradeoffs between hardware costs and software costs (see below). A computer that is programmed once, at whatever cost, can then be replicated without further software expenditure. However, frequent programming changes (and consequent debugging) are expected in a *general-purpose* environment. Here a microcomputer may not be able to compete with a larger system. Micro systems may also be relatively short of sophisticated operating systems, programming languages and debugging facilities. In some circumstances it is easier and cheaper to get the required results using a minicomputer. This is only to emphasise that available microcomputers are not miracle 'cure-alls'. They need to be evaluated, in common with all other competing systems, according to cost and performance in a given application context.

The success of integrated circuitry is resulting in an ever-widening applications base. More and more manufactured products are designed on the assumption that they will carry computing power in microelectronics. In many instances there is more memory or computing capability on a single chip than is required for an application. This circumstance necessarily encourages the designer to look at the product afresh, to see how an enhanced design could exploit available microelectronics potential.

Product design, taking chip potential into account, can also improve product quality and extend product life. Additional microcomputers can be incorporated in a product to enhance reliability by providing a back-up capability; or micros can interact in the same device to provide a composite (or joint) result. A consequence of these and related trends is that computers are increasingly being involved in the design process itself. Drafting tasks in the design of integrated circuits can be extremely tedious. Making a 100,000-gate array can involve the precise placement of around half a million rectangles. Computers are good at this sort of activity. The diminishing costs of microprocessors and their increasing power are making them attractive in many jobs formerly performed by people.

A designer should evaluate microprocessor potential with care. When contemplating using a micro in a specific application, the designer should ask questions about the micro impact on design flexibility, product value, required number of components, costs, the degree of control over the process, and the effect of the microprocessor on the user's or operator's job. It may be that design flexibility is enhanced, but at high cost (because of a need for excessive software effort or for some other reason). Or it may be that very significant cost savings can be achieved, but only by sacrificing some flexibility in task performance.

Having decided to opt for a microprocessor-based design, the engineer may start at a relatively basic level, choosing to build the microcomputer system round the selected microprocessor chip. This can involve much time and effort, and may only be justified where a large number of systems are to be built for one particular application (for example, in the manufacture of television games, process controllers, and electronic control systems for cars). Design at this level can involve the addition of interface circuits, development of software, testing of hardware and software as a total system, and the final packaging of the system as a commercially attractive product. And it can be extremely difficult even to evaluate the basic microprocessor prior to configuring the system from the individual component level.

If only a few systems are to be built for an application, it is rarely cost-effective to configure microprocessor systems at the component level. With only a few systems required, the high development costs will still be much in evidence when spread over the small number of units. In some cases there may be reasons, even in a poor cost-effective situation, why design should start with component configuration around the microprocessor.

With low production runs (say, in tens rather than thousands), the designer is likely to opt for available computer modules carrying interface circuits and memory. Some packaged micro-computers are focussed on particular applications and can be purchased as well defined elements in the design of a system. Again it is important to look at available software: software development costs can be the main factor in determining the final price of a microprocessor-based product.

A consequence of increased microprocessor availability is that the designer is more able to concentrate on overall systems considerations. The 'circuit diagram' has been represented as, in effect, the program which dedicates the universal logic component (the microprocessor) to a specific task at a specific time. In this sense the designer works in appropriate circumstances with fixed hardware: once the microcomputer configuration is settled, a prototype system can be produced quickly upon completion of the necessary software.

To maximise the design impact of microprocessors it is necessary to appreciate the characteristics of selected micros, those of available chips in the family, and the availability of relevant microprocessor development systems. It is helpful to develop software on a modular or structured basis to aid debugging and so reduce development time. In hardware development, input/output (I/O) logic receives early consideration. Other critical areas, particularly ones involving complex functions, may be expected to receive the engineer's attention in the early design stages. Initial design may be followed by prototype evaluation, small-number construction for field testing, and large-scale production where this is appropriate.

Design using microprocessor-based systems allows improvement of functional systems based on hardwired logic (or other conventions), the supplanting of costlier processing devices, and the development of new products formerly prohibited by processor sizes and costs. An early example (1975) of improvement of existing industrial products related to engine transducers. These have traditionally been selected for stability and linearity. The advent of microprocessors made it possible to trade off transducer performance against new processor capabilities. It was found that microprocessors could cope with stability factors and other parameters. Other early examples related to interfacing with such devices as teleprinters and tape printers (interface provisions were incorporated into microprocessor software).

Costly processing systems (for example, some types of business system) have now been supplanted by designs based on microcomputers, a circumstance that may be regarded as illustrative of a general trend: micros have facilitated the design of relatively cheap systems with a high level of processing capability. At the same time, a wide range of new products based on machine intelligence have been designed, produced and made available in the market (see Chapter 5). Just as there are several levels of design in the microprocessor environment, so there are several distinct ways in which design using microprocessors can impinge on the market scene.

PROJECT CONTROL

There are various stages in the design and development procedure. It is important that these be identified and given the necessary attention. The proportion of the total project time devoted to any particular stage depends upon the level of design and the application in question.

An initial requirement is to define the purpose of the project. Good answers to the wrong problems are not helpful. When the problem has been defined it is possible to describe the system (and subsystems) needed to solve it. During design and development, changes will be introduced to the system specification: there should be mechanisms to cope with such modifications. It is also necessary to anticipate the required provisions for maintenance of the functional system. The development of a successful microprocessor-based application depends upon the right mix of various activities: systems design, programming, electronics assembly, etc. The various activities should be organised according to effective project management.

There are evident trends towards cheap microprocessor hardware and cheap utility programs. However, there are still relatively costly areas in microprocessor system development. A non-standard facility could be expensive, as could the development of particular software items. Extensive testing is required at various stages for both hardware and software. It may be found, at any particular stage, that a particular mix of hardware (or of hardware and software) is inefficient or unworkable. This could lead to unanticipated and expensive development effort. It is sometimes tempting to cut corners in hardware design, assuming that flexible software will overcome any shortcomings. This can be a disastrous approach: software may be able to do the job, but may take too long. Costs permitting, good design should be attempted at each hardware, software and systems stage in the development project.

We have seen that the development projects for microprocessors relate to various classes of applications:

– hardwired logic substitution;

– minicomputer substitution;

– new roles and products.

The class of application helps to determine the character of the development project. However, most projects have features in common: we have already discussed the need to define problems and to optimise the various design activities. In most instances there is interaction, during the various phases of the development project, between the customer and the supplier. The functional and legal terms of this interaction should be made clear. Contractual responsibilities should be defined, with attention to such considerations as party obligations, copyright, software indemnities, etc. It is also necessary to define the required operation and performance level of the product. The parties may disagree on when development may be regarded as complete.

A detailed product specification should be formulated, allowing for the possibility of later modification and enhancement. A specification of inputs and outputs facilitates the drawing up of a programme of tests to check out the system at a later stage in development. Attention should also be given to the operating environment of the system. How will it be physically housed and sited? Will it accept wide variations of temperature and humidity? Should it be expected to tolerate vibration? And it is also necessary to define the various support provisions, the facilities for documentation, maintenance and training.

When the character of the problem and the features of the system intended to solve it have been defined (together with the necessary legal and environmental issues), it is appropriate to begin the various stages of design and development. Principal tasks include: device selection; looking to the various hardware/software tradeoffs; reliability and testing; and the various design activities peculiar to the requirements of a particular application. (These various tasks are profiled below. See also Chapter 3 for a profile of software development.) Effective project control – defining the project stages, allocating resources, supervising schedules, etc – should be applied at all times to the overall design and development procedure. This procedure begins with recognition of the problem and application requirement, and ends with incorporation of enhancements to a functionally successful system.

DEVICE SELECTION

The approach to device selection is determined by the level of design. It can be assumed that designers of microprocessor-based systems will rely on components available on the market: they will leave design of new microprocessor architectures and new ROMs and RAMs to the components manufacturers. The use of microprocessors in design can be considered at three hardware levels:

- at the *component* level, systems can be configured using microprocessor chips and memory chips for specific applications;

- at the *card* or *board* level, the microprocessor will be already linked to RAM, ROM, I/O devices, to form the basic microcomputer;

- at the *chassis* or *boxed* level, a system is provided complete with microprocessors cards, memories, power supplies, ancillary devices, etc.

It is important to distinguish between the three levels. What may be economic at one level, in certain circumstances, may not be economic at another. Cost, as well as the intended application, is highly relevant to the level at which design begins. Where a system is to be replicated thousands of times, it will almost certainly be better to design the system from components. Where few versions of the system are required, a card or boxed system may suffice. It is worth considering the three design levels in more detail.

Component Level

An advantage in designing at the component level is that the engineer can exploit new component devices quickly as they appear on the market. Using manufacturers' literature the designer can employ a new ROM or RAM device before it is formalised in a new commercial board or boxed system. Awareness of new component products with enhanced performance characteristics necessarily increases the engineer's design capability.

One design example is where a prototype has been completed and a second system is being developed (*Microprocessors,* June 1978, pp 116–117). An electronic module was required in a special cash register application. Use was made of an 8085 chip, a complete 'computer-on-a-chip'. Four I/O wires from the chip drive a decode chip which in turn drives displays and a keyboard matrix. The device cycles around the displays, pausing at each for

250 µS. On every fourth cycle, the output from the keyboard matrix is read into the chip. The system has RAM and PROM.

The design has led to a saving of components. Use of a cassette interface chip is a cost-effective way of interfacing to a serial recording device. Minimisation of the number of components, through design at the component level, has achieved a high degree of reliability (inversely proportional to the number of components).

Card Level

At this level it is possible to buy a 'custom special', a configured microcomputer with certain defined characteristics and suitable for particular applications. Ideally it would fit neatly into the system; more likely, it would require some modification to meet requirements. Also, unit costs would be high if the production run was small. Invariably there is a critical point, depending upon the card complexity and the number of devices to be manufactured, at which the cost of a custom special equals the cost of a system configured from standard chips.

In one application, a card device was employed to aid the automatic testing of electric motors. A data module was required to initiate the tests, to determine the value of the results, to display the results on a VDU, and to accumulate the information on floppy disk. The design was effectively tailored by selecting the Intel 8080 SBC 80/10 single-card computer, an I/O card, two cards to control the disk, and an A/D card. This system provides an automatic testing facility and the generation of data for future analysis.

There are some physical constraints on choice of cards. For example, choice of a particular microcomputer card family involves commitment to a particular card size and shape. It is theoretically possible to mix different card form factors, but generally impractical to do so in a production environment. Some companies employ standard card forms, whereas others do not. The Zilog Z80-MCB microcomputer series, for example, is based on a standard card form, and other companies manufacture Zilog-compatible cards. Where non-standard cards are produced, there may be good reason. For example, the number of available connections to a card configuration may be increased by altering card shape or the positions of particular connections. Zilog cards, for example, being smaller than Intel cards, afford less space for connectors.

Chassis Level

At the chassis level we meet 'complete systems'. Hardware is purchased as a *boxed* or *packaged* system, similar in appearance to some microcomputers. The requirement then is to develop the necessary software. For example, the PDP-11/03 is a packaged microprocessor version of the DEC PDP-11 series of minicomputers. It connects to a dual floppy disk, a VDU, and a high-speed printer. In one specific database application there are also a paper-tape reader and a paper-tape punch.

In this application the aim was to model failure rates on complex electronic equipment. Data is fed in, punched out, stored on disk, and checked for validity. There is provision for editing on the VDU. Reliability statistics are compiled, and particular items of data can be retrieved from the database. This application indicates one area where microcomputers are encroaching on a traditional mainframe province. Use is made of a sophisticated software package and the relational database approach. The microcomputer may be regarded as a 'black box' device, prepackaged and suitable for particular defined purposes.

The chassis assembly or box that holds a set of selected cards is sometimes called a 'cage'. Guides hold each card in place on two of its four sides, with a connector on the chassis mounted perpendicular to the guides. The card edge carrying 'fingers' seats in the connector, being secured there by a locking bar in vibration-prone environments. Power can then be applied to the caged device, with I/O connections made to custom interfaces. The entire assembly is then usually installed in a commercially attractive enclosure with front panel, connectors, and other means of interaction with the user and the larger application system.

Specific Products

Particular micro models can be assessed, to some extent, by scrutinising the comparative specifications (Chapter 2) or by rigorous operational testing (see below). In some cases, a particular microprocessor may be the obvious choice for a particular application: it may, for example, have been used similarly before. In other instances, selection may involve compromise and the need for hardware modification.

Some system elements may be effectively specified by other system features. For example, necessary power supplies are defined by the requirements of individual cards. Total power requirements can be ascertained by adding up the needs of individual circuits.

Individual power requirements can be listed to yield the overall system power consumption. There are well over 1000 suppliers of power supplies for microcomputers. Some supplies are standardised to a particular chassis or rack size, whereas others are produced as modules to be built into items of equipment.

Some power supplies have integral cooling fans: some micro-computers produce as much heat as a 100-watt light bulb. Circuits adversely affected by over-heating can be difficult to locate, since when the cabinet is opened for access, the resultant cooling makes the fault go away.

Cost considerations often determine the choice of components, and component expenditure can follow choice of language for a particular system. For example, extra RAM is required to accommodate a compiler. A system using 64 kilobytes of RAM in mid-1978 cost more than $20,000. Such considerations may influence a designer's attitude to the choice of a compiled language.

It is relatively straightforward to choose between a ROM and a PROM in terms of basic costs, once program size and the production run have been decided. It is possible to chart respective ROM and PROM costs, taking into account masking charges, size of required memory, number of systems to be built, etc. Possible hidden costs should be contemplated. For example, a specified ROM pattern might contain errors, with subsequent necessary debugging costing hundreds of pounds in extra testing. In summary, PROMs always cost more than comparable ROMs, taking into account masking charges. A PROM may be regarded as cost-effective in quantities below a certain unit level. Cost factors inevitably influence the component selection philosophy, though economics do not always have the decisive impact. Application problems may be better solved with higher investment.

HARDWARE/SOFTWARE TRADEOFFS

Hardware and software combine to form the total system. Complex hardware provisions may simplify the software needed to satisfy the applications requirements. Conversely, sophisticated software may overcome hardware shortcomings, but at some cost. For a particular project there is an optimum hardware/software balance designed to solve the defined problems in a cost-effective way.

In microprocessor system design it is often necessary to make compromises between factors such as speed, cost, program size, number of packages and operational flexibility. Various formulae have been developed to aid the designer in creating the best adjustment of software to hardware (and vice versa). One factor is the cost of software generation, ie the total costing of writing, testing and debugging a program for the UK, the US and elsewhere. Total software costs can be given for programs of a known number of bytes, with total investment spread over the production volume for the system. Then hardware costs must be estimated.

Hardware costs tend to be small compared with expenditure on software development, but increase with large production runs. Software costs diminish with the size of the run. Clearly, any estimate of hardware/software tradeoffs must take into account the size of the intended market.

A hardware solution may be completed in less time, but software provides flexibility. With a software approach a functional description should lead to a modular partitioning of software for arrangement into a top-down hierarchy. If software is first written in a general code it can be translated later into the specific machine language of the microprocessor: this allows initial programming to be machine-independent. Hardware design should also begin with specific modules (gates, registers, etc) and focus on logical flow. Circuit considerations can be dealt with later.

In one example, it is required to design a UART (universal asynchronous receiver/transmitter) into a system for data handling purposes (*Electronic Design*, 13/9/78, pp 107–109). Parallel data bytes from an 8080 CPU are transferred back and forth by the UART and an external device. Other system requirements have been stated, and the hardware and software approaches discussed. Even in the simple UART example it is difficult to assess the various tradeoffs. Particular respective advantages in the hardware and software approaches are difficult to define in cost terms. In more sophisticated systems there is a greater number of hardware/ software possibilities: particular tradeoff features are even harder to evaluate for cost. At the same time it is acknowledged that determining the optimum boundary line between hardware and software is a critical design task. Design engineers in the micro-computer environment have to be intimately acquainted with both hardware and software possibilities.

RELIABILITY AND TESTING

Reliability of both components and design is essential to effective systems implementation. Testing, at various stages, is a crucial element in the design and development procedure, the quality of testing largely determining the success of the project. This implies that appropriate resources should be devoted to the testing of individual components, subsystems, software and the overall system.

Microprocessor chips and related components can fail for various reasons. There may be faults due to poor fabrication techniques or bad handling. Oxide faults are well known in MOS circuits, and in configured systems there can be assembly- and package-related failures. Individual components – microprocessors, memories, I/O circuits, etc – have unique failure mechanisms, as well as mechanisms in common with other devices. Some types of failure relate to the technology of manufacture of the device. Typical causes of chip-related failure are: photolithographic defects, oxide/junction contaminants, metallization faults, diffusion defects, mechanical faults and shortcomings in design.

In one categorization, failure modes can be *catastrophic* or *soft*. Catastrophic failure, caused by such things as oxide rupture and wire-bend failure, is abrupt and unambiguous. Soft failure may be hard to detect, only evident under particular operating conditions. In memories, soft failures usually only involve single bits and occur because of slow access, loss of data or multiple addressing. Some soft failures are related to the interaction between hardware and software.

It is difficult to test a microprocessor to ensure that it has no shortcomings for all possible conditions of use. Testing is complex for various reasons: the microprocessor's random logic nature; the bus system; the chip layout; and the relationship between software and hardware. A preliminary test program may be followed by a more sophisticated version. One common test approach is to subject a device sample to combinations of supply voltages, temperatures, timing conditions and parametric varia- tions. Worst case patterns with supply and timing variations can be applied to the device to determine failure modes and to reveal its performance under the most severe conditions. Screening tests can be used to detect a wide range of failure mechanisms. Tests such as visual examination, stabilization bake, thermal cycling, centrifuge, X-ray and vibration can determine failure mechanisms of various types (eg substrate mounting defects, bulk silicon defects, particle contamination, thermal mismatch, etc).

It is sometimes argued that microprocessors and other related integrated circuits are too complex to test: it cannot be said that any particular LSI microcircuit will definitely work under all its design conditions. IBM has tried to tackle the problem by stipulating two major testing objectives: to arrange for any logic circuit to be tested in a single operation; and to design circuits to be tested at lower than normal operation rates. These principles derive from the fact that an exhaustive test of a complex circuit is not possible because of time constraints; and simple slow-rate 'on or off' tests do not prove that devices will operate as required.

The approach follows Hewlett-Packard experience: it searched fruitlessly for a memory chip that would work to certain standards, but was finally forced to develop circuits that could tolerate faults. These circumstances, relevant to minicomputer circuits, related to pattern sensitivity: the chip failed only when a certain sequence of data patterns was fed to certain address locations. On a microprocessor, it is not the data pattern, but the program instruction sequence, which is critical.

To test a chip properly it should be possible to test each small section of logic. However, it is rarely possible to isolate the individual parts of the circuit, and some observers have noted that chips are not designed to be tested. One consequence is that testers can be disproportionately expensive: prices of £100,000 and more have been quoted. With increasingly complex microprocessor devices arriving on the market, the testing problem is unlikely to diminish. One approach is via wafer-scale self-testing.

Some test system manufacturers add large buffer memories able to drive, and be driven by, the microprocessor under test. The memories can be preloaded with serial instruction sets and run at processor speed. The device testers are required to monitor the control lines and to adjust the speed as the microprocessor handles different instructions. The test hardware can be speed controlled, but only programmable timing control can test marginal time situations within the processor. Some test systems carry multiprocessors able to control the high-speed buffer memories.

Lengthy tests are necessary to detect all possible failures. For example, a diagnostic program for the 8080 for the Sentry VII tester is about 11,000 clock cycles long. It exercises all of the 8080's 243 unique instructions with a total of 1377 tests. Some instructions are checked once, others many times. Honeywell has bought several Fairchild Sentry VIIs to test microprocessors.

Hewlett-Packard, using the 6800 microprocessor in various new instruments, does not perform incoming tests. Instead, the full board carrying the new device is tested using a logic-board tester. This approach is also followed by other companies, eg Racal-Dana, using 4004s in the series 9000 counter-timer. This company has found that the ROMs fail more often than the CPU, and that volumes are low enough to test the whole board.

In one categorization, there are five approaches used to the testing of microprocessors: in-system, comparison, algorithm-based, stored-response, and logic-board testers. The first two techniques are likely to be employed by low-volume users, the last two by commercial testers.

The most common testers are Fairchild's Sentry series (the Sentry VII is based on the FST-2 24-bit minicomputer), the Tektronix S-3260, and the Macrodata MD-501 (the cheaper MD154 is a subset of the 501). The M10A tester from Micro Control is based on the 8080 microprocessor, and generates algorithmic patterns at rates up to 10 MHz, using a floppy disk as mass memory. This programmed system can vary dc voltages, timing and other parameters, under software control. Increasingly, low-cost testers are available on the market.

There is a growing need for debugging aids for both hardware and software in microprocessor systems. Lack of powerful in-circuit debugging support is still a problem to digital designers, and systems often fail because of inadequate testing provisions. Various descriptions of the problem, and approaches to solving it, are given in the literature (see bibliography). Again, the designer is presented with a 'multilevel' problem. It is one thing to test a bought-in microprocessor device, another to test the developed system in which it is a single hardware component. 'Development systems' have been designed to test hardware and software to-gether, based on various approaches (eg simulator, microcomputer with program monitor, and microcomputer with hardware console): these have the aim of isolating the symptoms, aiding diagnosis and correcting the faults.

The engineer needs to acquaint himself with the various testing techniques and development/debugging aids, and to decide which of these are most appropriate to the various stages of the design project in question.

OTHER DESIGN CONSIDERATIONS

A major stimulus to design innovation is the introduction of new components on the market. New ROMs, RAMs, processors, clocks, etc, can facilitate a wide range of unprecedented system designs —

which is why engineers make efforts to keep in touch with manufacturers' brochures, the technical press, and other sources of up-to-date information. New products can also simplify existing designs. The introduction of new programmable LSI interface circuits, for example, made it possible to use far fewer components in the design of systems based on the 8080 microprocessor.

Some manufacturers supply *design kits* to aid design prototyping. The SDK-80 was an early kit of this sort supplied by Intel. It contained a basic 8080 system (CPU, RAMs, EPROMs and peripheral circuits), a printed circuit board (with discrete components and other hardware), and design and operating manuals. The Intellec MDS (microcomputer development system) and the ICE-80 in-circuit emulator subsystem were used to provide software and hardware development support. The ICE-80 module facilitated debugging in the operating environment, with all operations of the system bus controlled and analysed through the MDS console.

Today a wide range of design and development aids are available from manufacturers. We have already mentioned Motorola's Exorcizer, containing a complete M6800 operating system and built-in firmware to help the designing and debugging of prototype systems. The basic Exorcizer consists of three boards, a power supply and chassis. The microprocessor board carries processor, clock, bus control logic, clock control circuit and buffers. Firmware on the debug module consists of the Exbug loader/diagnostic program. Similar facilities are available in association with the wide range of micro products from other manufacturers.

Some component products lend themselves readily for incorporation in microprocessor system designs; others, perhaps with singular advantageous features, may be more difficult to use. Dynamic RAMs, for example, provide about four times the data packing density of static memories, and may be regarded as good candidates for design. At the same time, there are problems about access timing requirements and selection of memory-refresh facilities. In some systems it is also more economic to use static devices, eg in ones requiring less than 8K bytes of memory. In larger systems, dynamic RAMs are economic. There is a 'grey area', between system requirements of about 8K bytes and about 16K bytes, where a number of considerations − cost, ease of design, number of components, etc − determine the final choice. Factors such as memory speed and memory refresh are discussed in the literature (eg *Electronic Design*, 26/4/78, pp 84−92).

Designers also need to choose between competing system architectures and technologies when developing complex devices. For example, two approaches are possible in the development of devices for use in computer systems such as CPU's, memory controllers, floppy disk controllers, and high-speed fixed- or moving-head disk controllers. The designer may opt for straightforward medium-scale integration (MSI) logic elements. An alternative, more flexible approach relies on bipolar microprocessor: supplementary hardware is minimized and functional control is placed in microprogram memory. Engineers need to compare these two approaches in implementing microprogrammable hardware for sophisticated data processing applications.

There are particular advantages to the designer in both fixed-instruction and bit-slice bipolar microprocessors. The former are self-contained and easy-to-use. They are suitable for medium- and high-speed control applications. The latter are suitable for high-speed applications requiring a large amount of arithmetic capability and for designs requiring specially tailored microprocessor functions. These differences must be fully understood by the design engineer.

Other considerations relate to component matching and compatibility, fault-tolerant design, and efficient use of cycle time. It is possible, for example, to use 'cycle-stealing' peripheral devices in circumstances where a microprocessor's buses remain unused for a significant part of the instruction time. An approach of this sort allows the processor to concentrate on program-controlled real-time tasks. Criteria for cycle-stealing and details of the cycle-stealing sequence can be established in a particular applications context.

Choice of bus systems is also important in the design approach. Again the engineer must balance ease of design against costs. The use of a standard bus can aid the design of systems: it may be possible simply to plug in a few cards and to program appropriately. But if a standard bus is used in every item in a large production run, unit costs may be unreasonably high. If the run is, say, less than one hundred, it is likely that use of a standard bus (see Chapter 1) is justified by the cost savings during the design phase.

Bus systems tend to be more expensive than specialized systems, requiring a higher number of integrated circuits. To cope with the required number of possible configurations, the bus design may incorporate an 'overkill' element. However, use of a bus removes the need to redesign a configuration: you simply pull out one card and insert others, providing that the new requirement is similar to the old. An applications example would be the design of process control interfaces used in petrochemical plants. Since the applications are similar, it is possible to transfer the bulk of hardware and software experience from one job to the next. Maintenance and upgrading of systems is also facilitated. If performance is found to be too slow, a faster processor card or memory card can be plugged in. An enlarged micro (say, a new 16-bit design) can be used, providing the necessary compatibility requirements are met.

It should not be expected that all the phases in the design and development project will progress smoothly. The various stages – definition of problem, definition of system and subsystems, hardware design and software development, testing and debugging, maintenance and system enhancement, etc – all have both unique and common trouble-spots and bottlenecks. It is important to be aware of the sorts of things that can go wrong.

There may be difficulty in obtaining components from a manufacturer or supplier. This may be because of unexpected fabrication problems, particularly likely with innovatory and sophisticated devices. Or there may be prolonged industrial action. It may be that selected (and available) components and cards do not work in the ways implied by the manufacturers' literature. Documentation may be inadequate for this or other reasons (it is a constant complaint of technical authors that project estimates rarely allow for adequate documentation expenditure). It may be that the documentation is simply loose or ambiguous about how a product works. The user may have made unjustified assumptions about device performance.

Software development facilities may be inadequate: a project may have been started without prior appreciation of what aids were available. It may also happen that, through underestimating the software requirement, the final developed programs will not fit into the available memory. When configuring a system at the chip level it is essential to provide enough memory. At board level, it may be prudent to allow the contingency of an extra RAM or ROM board. Finally, it may be found that the fully developed operating system does not meet the original functional specification: the subsystems may simply not combine to fit the bill. If the shortfall is significant it may be necessary to redesign from scratch, with all the expense that this implies. Some operational discrepancy from specification may be expected. Hopefully, minor modifications will meet the requirements.

Ideally, high-level staff will be employed on the design project. It is a tautology, though worth stating, that the most competent staff will achieve the best results. Problems sometimes arise where too many people are employed on a design and development project. However good the on-going documentation, the designers take certain assumptions 'as read' or 'as understood'. Where the assumptions, from one person to another, are incompatible all sorts of problems can arise. This possibility further emphasises the importance of comprehensive documentation at every stage.

It is also advisable to use well supported products, with back-up from the manufacturer if anything goes wrong. Some observers rate this consideration as more important than microprocessor performance features such as storage behaviour or speed. Designers are well advised to keep hardware development and software development separate, until the time when they have to be combined. It can be very confusing to try to run undebugged software on undebugged hardware. The fully developed software should be loaded onto the machine at a late stage.

Adequate time should be allocated to implementation and testing (one suggestion is that for every man-day spent in design there is a saving of two man-days in implementation). Unique problems can become apparent when the system is transferred to its operating environment. The only useful test of the success of a project is how well (in terms of cost and performance) the system solves the application problem in question.

SOME DESIGN APPLICATIONS

Microprocessors are being used in an ever-increasing range of applications (see Chapter 5). Some design consequences in selected fields are briefly indicated.

Process control systems are more efficient and easier to use because of micros. Microprocessor controllers in a distributed configuration provide more power in this context than does a large minicomputer. Furthermore, a microprocessor-based distribution system can improve performance by working at the process-control valves.

A Powell Industries (Houston) process-control system uses controller microprocessors in multiple control loops to serve as a virtual large minicomputer. The new Micon microprocessor controllers supervise eight loops per unit, with communication links to a central operator's CRT. The Micons are preprogrammed to control their loops by means of 45 sophisticated control functions. There is no need for supervisory or optimization control by a larger computer.

A digital communication and control system from Xomax Corporation puts the microprocessors at the control valves, thus replacing many field cables by a few data highways. The micros provide proportional, integral and derivative control. If the Xomax systems fails, the controllers continue to operate according to their last optimized set point. Hence control is more effective and more reliable.

Foxcal, relevant to the designer who wants laboratory results in the form of graphic plots, is a video-oriented interpretive language that uses the instruction sets of Digital Equipment's Focal, developed for the PDP-8/11 range. Foxcal software makes it easier to design process controls, to assemble process control systems, and to verify performance. This software is particularly relevant to the use of micros in the process control environment.

(Various problems in trying to use microprocessors in the industrial and process control environment have been highlighted (*Electronics,* 25/5/78, pp 89–90). One difficulty is unproven microprocessors (the familiar testing problem). Another relates to device specifications: vendors produce a preliminary spec sheet and encourage design, but when the part arrives the specification has changed. Sometimes a particular micro may not have enough power for a particular recommended application, and to go for a larger micro may result in unjustified increases in unit costs. Designers in industrial control have sometimes complained about what the microprocessor industry is making available.)

Microprocessors are also influencing the design of local network systems in communications. The local network concept employs a standardized communications interface facilitating access to a random serial-data highway. The highway links via a single coaxial cable to all process computers in the network. Using a new name-assignment convention, processes can be requested through a network catalogue which provides the association between names and addresses.

Despite the difficulties in applying microprocessors in some application environments, they are having an impact in all areas where low-cost digital control is needed. Ship-borne radars, for example, are required to convert variable location, coordinates to a fixed-reference coordinate system. In one application of this sort a Monolithic Memories MM1 5701/6701 chip was selected to ease the load on the radar's CPU. The LSI bit-slice processor is an ALU plus a 16-word register file combined in a 40-pin package. The instruction set contains all the steps needed for the required computations.

Other applications of microprocessors in digital control have occurred in such areas as:

— teleprinter redesign;

— echo sounding;

— display terminals;

— blood analysis;

— cash registers;

— television games;

— bulk weighing;

— process control.

The list could easily be extended. A central design consequence has been that microprocessors have forced engineers to re-examine overall equipment design. It is tempting to think of ways in which the potential of micros, introduced originally to provide basic digital control, could be exploited in enhanced equipment facilities.

MULTIPROCESSORS

There is a growing trend towards the use of multiprocessor systems based on microprocessors. It is often an attractive design option to use multiple processors to meet performance requirements. Improvements can be achieved in throughput, reliability, real-time response, and modular system expansion capabilities. As with most microprocessor design options it is possible to design multiprocessors from scratch, or to purchase off-the-shelf multiple processor microcomputer systems (eg the Intel SBC 80/05 and 80/20).

Improved performance capability can be achieved by arranging for each of several microprocessors to handle separately particular system tasks. A multiple processor bus structure allows new processors to be added to the system in modular fashion, further facilitating task partitioning. The Intel MULTIBUS, for example, supports multiprocessor systems with its multimaster bus arrangement. It is necessary to arrange priority sequences for use of bus facilities: distinctions can be made between serial (daisy-chain) bus arbitration and parallel (hardware-encoded) bus arbitration.

Software operations, essential to multiprocessor working, include *mutual exclusion, communication,* and *synchronization.* Mutual exclusion supervises the correct allocation of common memory and peripherals, a necessary provision to prevent mix up of data being handled by different processors. Communication allows a program running on one processor to send data to, or receive data from, a program running on another processor. It is normal for two processors to communicate through buffers in common storage. Synchronization is a special case of communication. A program may be 'turned on' by receipt of a synchronization signal: the 'wake-up' signal causes a 'sleeping' program to resume execution. Mutual exclusion is necessary to use of synchronization signals.

There are various ways of improving the performance of a microcomputer system. For example, additional memory and I/O devices may be added. The multiprocessor option suggests the addition of further microprocessors. Mainframe multiprocessors are well established (eg the IBM 360/65 and the Univac 1108), and it can be argued that the case is even stronger for micro multiprocessors. Hierarchical multiprocessors are feasible also, with sub-processors serving other processors at a higher level.

Most types of microprocessors can be connected in multiprocessor arrays: in some cases there can be awesome design problems. Even where a micro may be relatively unsuitable for multiprocessor operation, its cheapness may justify use in this way. An example is the 8080A, with inferior interrupt handling capability to more sophisticated microprocessors. When, for example, more than three 8080s are connected to the same memory bus, the average speed of each processor is decreased. However, the overall system speed is still higher than it would be for a single-CPU system.

The UK National Physical Laboratory has announced that it is teaming with Scicon to develop a multi-mini/microcomputer system called Demos. Up to 100 computers could be linked via an 8-million-word-per-second parallel ring. Such systems, it is argued, allow expansion, flexibility in matching computers to a required response speed, and low cost in comparison with time-shared minicomputers and mainframes. A number of multiprocessor systems are being developed along similar lines.

Multiprocessor techniques have been demonstrated in various mainframe areas. For example, ICL's distributed array processor uses an array of simple processing elements in the memory of a conventional mainframe computer. Telecommunications is a further significant applications area. Systems Reliability, with Warwick University, is developing a multiprocessor system as a universal interface processor in data communications. The system is based on the Texas Instruments 9900 16-bit microprocessor.

Other systems are more experimental, less focussed on a particular type of application. One research programme, for example, aims to define a multiprocessor architecture where the communication network within the system is not a bottleneck.

5   The Application Spectrum

INTRODUCTION

Microprocessors are now being used in thousands of applications: it is hard to think of any industrial or commercial area not already affected by the 'microprocessor revolution'. In the literature — technical and popular — microprocessors are 'ubiquitous' and 'all-pervasive'. Journalists head their pieces with suitable catchlines — 'Hello, Mr Chips', 'Chip In, Everybody', 'Chips with Everything' (this last in one publication after another). There can be no doubting that, in less than a decade, microprocessors have encroached on almost every area of modern technological society — from sewing-machines to vast automated factories, from toys to interplanetary probes, from watches to traffic control.

A recent Department of Industry publication (*Microelectronics, The New Technology*) divided applications areas into five general categories:

— enhancement of existing products (including domestic appliances, vehicles, lift controls, cash registers, defence systems, etc);

— new types of product (including word processors, miniature television, electronic pianos, personal computers, etc);

— industrial and other control systems (including applications under seven heads — continuous process plant, machinery, electrical goods, materials handling, transport, medical engineering, and agriculture);

— data processing (including pay accounting, order processing, banking transactions, production scheduling, library control, etc);

— new products or new techniques in communications (including data communications equipment, telemetry, electronic typesetting, remote terminals in shops and banks, electronic

99

funds transfer, etc).

There is an arbitrary element in any particular breakdown of the applications areas. Writers are partly influenced by available information and their own interests. If headings are too general, it is difficult to provide a balanced profile of the areas they denote; if headings are too specific, the heading-list is impossibly cumbersome. The present chapter briefly describes microprocessor applications under fifteen headings. It is one possible breakdown among many, and there is inevitable overlap between the areas:

- Simple Digital Control;
- Business and Offices;
- Automation, Process Control;
- Robotics;
- Cars;
- Aerospace;
- Printing and Printers;
- PoS, Cash Registers;
- Education;
- Medicine;
- Communications;
- Terminals;
- Instrumentation;
- Speech Synthesis, Voice Recognition;
- Games and Domestic.

SIMPLE DIGITAL CONTROL

The earliest and least sophisticated microprocessors were largely devoted to simple digital control applications. Typical micro usage of this sort includes provision of hotel wake-up calls, medical analysis of blood samples, and electronic games.

A frequent use of 4-bit microprocessors is as simple controllers. In one estimate, around 80% of all single-chip microcomputer applications will be as controllers, eg in petrol pumps. A description has been given of how the Intel 8048 can be used as a control element in a petrol pump. Here the microcomputer is required to perform five separate tasks: measurement of petrol dispensed, displaying of quantity dispensed and cost, control of pump valves and motors, allowing fuel type selection and pump status monitoring, and transmitting sale details to a central point.

In this application the 8048 has quasi bidirectional ports, ie the individual lines in a port can be inputs or outputs. One port is used as an input (for system reset) and an output (for motor control and communication with the central point). Another port controls the four pump valves. Instructions may be allocated to individual valves or one instruction may govern them all. The computation required in this application involves quantities – of petrol or cash – that can be conventionally handled in binary-coded-decimal form. The instructions should therefore be capable of handling BCD quantities.

Many companies have developed digital control systems based on microprocessors. Motorola, for example, has developed control provisions for lifts and air conditioning systems. In mid-1978, Barcrest, one of Europe's leading manufacturers of fruit machines, placed an order with Motorola for microprocessors worth more than £350,000. The M6800 micros – with the associated memories, logic and power control devices – were ordered for use in Barcrest's microprocessor-based games control systems employed in the fruit machines. This was one of the largest microprocessor orders outside the US.

Mostek has used the flexible 3872 single-chip microcomputer in many digital control applications. The device has 4032 bytes of ROM and 128 bytes of RAM, double the storage capacity of the earlier 3870. Applications include petrol pumps, point-of-sale terminals, push-button radios, and a wide range of domestic appliances.

BUSINESS AND OFFICES

The impact of microprocessors in the business environment has led to progressive development of the 'electronic office' concept. There are many ways in which micros are influencing the office scene. An increasing range of business sytems are microprocessor-based, and there are weekly announcements of new 'personal microcomputers', programmable calculators, and micro facilities for specific tasks such as VAT control and advertisement accounting. More and more word processing systems – from sophisticated and expensive models to small personal devices – are becoming available. A large number of companies are involved in the growing automated office market.

Programmable calculators, with increased power and potential, are having a growing impact on the business scene. They can in fact represent a cost-effective alternative to the use of time-sharing services. As one example, around 10,000 TI-59 programmable calculators are in use within the Texas Instruments organisation alone (with company time-sharing costs reduced by about 40 per cent). Typical applications include: pricing and order totalling; least cost analysis and estimates;production control; stock control; accounting; general management; investment and insurance, etc. (Perhaps more dramatically, the TI-58 and TI-59 calculators have been used by hot-air balloonists for navigational and endurance computations, by sailors in *The Observer* Round-Britain yacht race, and by the RAF in a training evaluation North Polar Flight.)

The Texas Instruments SR60A fills the gap between conventional programmable calculators and current personal computers. The device includes an intelligent calculator, a 'question/answer' prompting display, and a built-in thermal printer. The SR60A is well suited to small business where it is likely to be used by operators without special training in the use of computers. Betos Systems (Nottingham, UK) has developed a payroll package for the machine, and Abacas (Dublin) has produced a program for keeping track of bar stocks. The organisers of the 1978 Milk Race, the Tour of Britain cycle race, used the SR60A to provide instant printouts of the complex points system for results during the race.

There is a proliferation of personal computers for the business user. Some of these start at the low, 'hobbyist' end, where users assemble microcomputer kits for their own fun and experience. Mostly, business users require cheap functional systems in a completed form, and many of these are available (see bibliography). By late-1978 it was confidently predicted that microcomputers in business would soon reach deluge proportions. At that time, impressive models were already available, with 4000 bytes of memory, a keyboard, a CRT display and cassette recorder for about $600. It is estimated that the workload of a small business could be handled by systems costing less than $5000.

Many of the microcomputer stores, encouraging public access and interest, have made available new micro models for personal use. The Newbear Computing Store, for example, introduced the Panda personal computer in late-1978. It is based on the Motorola 6800 and features 8K bytes of read/write memory and 8K bytes of EPROM. A keyboard is provided for data entry, and a 9-in display can show 16 lines of 64 characters each. Interfaces for audio cassette are available, with a TTL-compatible parallel I/O board based on Motorola's peripheral interface adapter. As well as the normal 8K Basic facilities, the firmware interpreter offers multiple statements per line, cassette file handling, a Trace debugging facility, etc.

In late-1978, ICL began negotiations with Qume for daisy wheel printers as part of their development of a word processing potential. Word processing software has been developed for the 7502 series of terminals and the 1500 terminal inherited from Singer. It may be expected that an increasing proportion of these word processing facilities will be microprocessor-based. (It is also worth mentioning intelligent copiers, facsimile devices and other approaches to text handling.)

Microprocessor logic is seen as essential in maximising word processor potential. A wide range of micro-based products was shown at the 1978 International Word Processing Exhibition held in London. The available systems now have sophisticated facilities — layout optimisation, justification, editing, etc. Most of the products derive from the large companies such as Xerox, Rotaprint and Olivetti. Sometimes, however, a private individual may develop an interesting system: a case in point is Cy Endfield's Microwriter, described as a 'personal word processor'. The machine uses a chord keyboard and single-line display to record text into a built-in memory. The text can also be recalled and edited. Text is stored in an 8K byte CMOS RAM, and overall control is provided by an RCA Cosmac microprocessor. (Endfield: "This does for words and text what the pocket calculator did for the adding machine.")

Particular business functions and activities can be easily performed on micro-based systems: examples have been cited in connection with programmable calculators. Programs have been written to carry out VAT calculations on microcomputers. For example, programs have been written in TDL Disk Basic for use under the Digital Research operating system CP/M for Z80 microprocessor systems. As another example, ADS has been designed to monitor 2000 newspaper advertising linage contracts. It runs on an Altair 8800 with floppy disk, employing Altair Extended Disk Basic V 3.4. ADS can be modified for the contract fulfilment requirements of individual companies.

AUTOMATION, PROCESS CONTROL

Some of the most significant microprocessor applications are in factory automation (closely linked to Robotics — see below), process control, and other industrial areas. Again the examples are legion. Fuel-fired furnace variables can now be automatically controlled by microprocessors, as can machine-tools, car-production lines, electric power generation, etc. In furnace-variable control the microprocessor is preprogrammed with information regarding the type of fuel being used and the permissible oxygen levels. Complete control of a difficult environment is offered, with significant fuel cost savings (*Machinery*, 1/3/78, pp 25–27).

The increasing importance of microprocessor control of machine tools was shown at the PEP78 exhibition of control systems. As one example, the Vaughan (Systems and Programming) 4M system, based on the Texas Instruments TMS 9900 microprocessor, is seen as suitable for a wide variety of industrial control and automation processes. In one specific application, a microprocessor is used in threaded fastener control: for example, in the assembly of differential gear cases for large truck axles. Two air motors employed in the Power Tool Division of Rockwell International provide up to 850 ft-lb of torque for automatic and sequential tightening of fasteners. In particular, the tension is controlled by the microprocessor-based unit.

In 1978, the US consultancy, Frost and Sullivan, released a 234-page report forecasting that the microprocessor element in European process control installations would total $40 million by 1981 and $200 million by 1986. Figures were also given for the growth in process control for various European countries. Britain (120 per cent growth between 1976 and 1986) trailed West Germany (186), Belgium (182), France (147) and Italy (143).

The German process control systems house, COMPAC, developed the CMS 80-01, the first complete West German microcomputer system, in 1974. (By contrast, Siemens produced their first microcomputer for the 1977 Interkama exhibition.) The CMS 80-01, in a 27-in rack-mounted version, is based on micros from Intel and TI. Part of the attraction of micros in the process control environment is that they represent such a small proportion of the total systems cost.

A further benefit afforded by process control microprocessors is that they facilitate modular construction of control circuitry. This is relevant to the repair philosophy in a particular system. A process control system's *mean time to repair* is as important as its *mean time between failures.* Micros also allow automatic diagnosis of control circuit faults down to the module level, and automatic indication of diagnosis results. In one typical instance, a microcomputer module based on an 8080 processor has achieved a mean time to repair of only a few minutes with complex process-control equipment. Special software diagnostics allow even an untrained operator to test all the modules in less than a minute.

The 8080-based microcomputer can serve as a stand-alone device in a process-control system. Or it can interface input and output data to another computer (eg a Honeywell Level 6 mini-computer) in a two-level hierarchy. Many microcomputers may cluster around a mini, each micro able to run multiple tasks and to supply data to the minicomputer.

The diagnostics software package can be housed in PROM used to test the hardware modules and to store fault data for subsequent analysis. When PROM is loaded during manufacture, a cyclically redundant code is used to generate a parity check word for each kilobyte of ROM, the word being stored at the end of the 1K byte block. The check word is recomputed and compared with the one at the end of the memory segment, thus verifying memory integrity. Using methods of this sort, the microcomputer modules can be tested to an acceptable level in less than one minute: it is practical, for systems of this sort, to arrange for 80% of the hardware to be automatically testable for only 10% added cost.

Microprocessors are increasingly being employed in test instru-mentation in the process-control environment. An instrumentation controller, for example, governs a series of test instruments linked to its bus. The Systron Donner 3530 instrumentation controller is built around an 8080A and programmed in IEEE 488/BASIC for bus compatibility. The micro and standard bus facilitate control of up to fourteen compatible instruments (see also Instrumentation below).

Multiple microprocessor systems are applicable to the numerical control of machine tools: a key advantage is that the NC systems can be modular in both hardware and software. Function-specific software can be written, without concern for other operations. Microprocessors facilitate a distributed processing approach to the various machine tasks. Also, there are enhanced possibilities for operator/computer interaction, allowing the computers to assist rather than dominate the operation. This also helps operators to deal with unexpected cases and debugging requirements.

New products have exploited the relative cheapness of micro-processor-based control. C. E. Johansson, for example, has devel-oped a radio touch-probe and a microprocessor-based interface for use with a Sajo machining centre with automatic tool-change.

A number of the new devices are in production use in Sweden. The probe transmits a measured value, allowing the signal to be used to correct the machine tool for subsequent cuts. The probe, selected in the same way as a cutting tool, is powered by a 9V battery. The transmitted analogue radio signal is proportional to the amount by which the probe tip is deflected on contact with the workpiece.

Factory operations are increasingly being automated – from handling of raw materials, through machining and assembly, to warehousing and stock control (see also Robotics below). Automated (or partially operated) plants are in operation in the US, Japan and Europe, with Japan often represented as the world leader in the move to total automation. Highly automated plants throughout the world are now manufacturing automobiles, engines, earth movers, oilwell machinery, lifts, electrical equipment, machine tools and other products. Such plants are well on the way to practical realisation of the old dream of the fully automated factory.

An outstanding example of factory automation is the McDonnell Douglas parts fabrication plant in St. Louis. Two dozen acres of milling machines automatically cut and shape airframe parts to a 0.0025-in tolerance. A few men glance at control panels or sweep the cuttings. The effective control is achieved by a complex of programmable controllers, microcomputers, minicomputers and mainframes.

The various stages in the route to automated plant – digital control of machining, computer-assisted design, adaptive controls, etc – have yielded production processes that are more reliable, more productive, more economical (generating less scrap), and generally more efficient. Microprocessors have made a substantial contribution in this immensely important field. In all accounts the impact of microprocessors and chip technology in general is accelerating the inexorable trend towards 'unmanned manufacturing'.

Microcomputers are being used to carry out a broad range of industrial control tasks. For example, a hydroelectric plant in Alabama is entirely controlled, by means of microcomputers, from a control room of another plant 90 miles away. Three IMP-16C/200s from National Semiconductor are employed, performing various data acquisition and plant control tasks. The 'base' micro-computer supervises the two 'remotes', the three performing as an effective distributed system. Control routines are stored in

PROM, with RAM used for temporary storage of data.

Design based on microcomputers allowed the system to be developed on a single set of control subroutines. Hardwired logic would have necessitated hardware duplication for each generator.

Data acquisition is a central task of microcomputers in industrial applications, whether in power generation control, machine-tool supervision, or control of chemical plant. Plastic injection moulders are being controlled by micros, as are steel plants, welding processes in factories, and refining and other processes in the petrochemical industry. Data acquisition systems (or data 'loggers') are being used to guarantee shopfloor accuracy and to supervise quality-control programmes. In all these areas, microprocessors are an innovatory and increasingly influential factor.

In the agricultural industry, microprocessors are being used to drive tractors and to aid dairy management. One journal *(Personal Computing,* April 1978) presented a program called HARVEST (Heuristic Application for Reaping Vegetables Electronically Scheduled in Total). The program can take into account environmental and weather conditions, watering and pest-control factors, to aid effective gardening. This light-hearted (hobby) proposal is clearly relevant to large-scale agricultural decision-making that could be based on microcomputers.

ROBOTICS

Developments in robotics are clearly linked to trends in fabrication technology. Microprocessors are increasingly employed to aid the automation of welding, assembly and other industrial procedures. The trends were well illustrated at last year's Welding Engineering at Harrogate. Many companies exhibited automated equipment and two robots were demonstrated for the first time.

At the time of the 1978 exhibition, conventional friction welding could already be fully automated. The Welding Institute at Abington, sponsored by the Department of Industry and the Mechanical Engineering Machine Tool Requirements Board, has developed a technique of radial friction welding where a ring is grafted onto a shaft or tube. Automated turntables, capable of handling components of up to 50 lb, have been introduced by BOC's automatic welding division. In 1978 ESAB introduced the PAF 19 point tracking unit which uses a microcomputer to direct the welding torch along the joints.

ASEA IRV-6/6kg robots are used in Austria to weld bicycle frames, and in Sweden the same devices are employed to arc weld such components as generator frames, metal furniture and car parts. IRV-6 robots are also used at Leyland's Cowley plant, by Piaggio in Italy to weld bicycle frames, and by Citroen, Renault and Daimler-Benz on production lines. Unimation has more than two dozen robots employed on MIG arc welding in the US and Europe, and is testing prototypes of a portable model intended for shipyard and other thickplate work. The model can automatically move a welding torch in as many as five axes at once. Hall Automation is also manufacturing an arc welding robot. In all these devices, microelectronic intelligence is an essential feature.

The Science Research Council is considering various proposals for investing in robotics, and the Department of Industry has funded work conducted by the British Robot Association. It is evident that functional robots can be applied in many activity areas: they can be used in commercial and domestic environments, as well as on the factory floor. They can also aid the educational task, helping to develop an understanding of artificial intelligence in machine systems.

Some effective robots have initially been developed by engineering colleges. One example is the robot car designed at Rice University in Houston. The vehicle was designed to seek out a shining light, a task accomplished by means of an on-board Z80 microprocessor communicating with a PDP-11 minicomputer over a two-way digital radio link. The Z80, operated in an interrupt mode, handles the car's reflex movements. The PDP-11 makes real-time navigational decisions and can also improve the car's performance, ie it can generate a better path for the car to take on a second trip over the same course towards the light. If the car collides, or the light is lost, the Z80 takes over control and sorts out the situation before returning control to the PDP-11.

Only one of the computers can communicate with the car at any one time. There are only three control inputs – speed, direction and steering – and these, governed by a multiplexing scheme, can originate at either computer. The Z80 was selected as the on-board microprocessor because of its single 5V power supply requirement and its single-phase clock. The 8-bit Z80, controlling data selectors, decides which of the two computers is going to receive information from the car's sensors. It also stores all movement vectors associated with the car's travel, ie vectors indicating steering angle, travel direction, and the length of the accomplished route. The PDP-11, with superior computing power, may be regarded as the effective brain of the system.

Such projects, almost invariably deriving from the computing scope offered by microcomputers, illustrate how robots can be organised to solve functional problems. This has relevance to a wide range of tasks in industry, commerce, education, medicine, the domestic environment, etc.

CARS

Microprocessors are increasingly finding their way into the electrical systems of motor cars, though one persistent problem has been the rough environment under the car bonnet. Motorola and Texas Instruments have contracts to develop purpose-built microelectronic circuits for the industry. Microprocessors offer more effective control systems than can be achieved by other methods, providing environmental and other problems can be overcome.

Vehicle temperature and humidity vary widely, a circumstance that is likely to stress many microelectronic circuits beyond their limits. The Automobile Association has recorded a temperature of $120°C$ under a car bonnet, and at the other extreme cars have to start at temperatures as low as $-40°C$. At high temperatures, the failure rate of microprocessors increases, and this factor has to be considered in system design.

The Lagonda car, first shown at the 1976 Motor Show, uses several microprocessors plus solid-state displays, touch-operated switches, and other control devices. Reliability has not been impressive in such application areas, rapid improvements are likely on a relatively short timescale. Various areas where microprocessors might be used in car systems have been identified.

An early application is likely to be in engine management, in control of fuel injection and ignition. Microprocessors might also be used to replace the wiring loom in a vehicle by an electrical signalling system linked to dashboard instrumentation with solid-state speedometers and other dials. There may be applications in suspension control and in supervision of heating and ventilation. More fancifully, there may be scope for microprocessor-controlled anti-collision radar and route guidance.

Analogue computers have been used for various car applications; for example, in the Bosch and Bendix electronic fuel injection systems. Analogue designs were relatively easy to adjust during vehicle development. For the same reason, Chrysler used an analogue computer to govern its Lean Burn spark-adjustment system. In 1976 tests the device worked with 99.9% reliability on 60,000 cars. In 1979 the system is available on all Chrysler's eight-cylinder engines. Analogue systems have also been employed by such companies as Volvo and Saab.

Some car systems combine analogue and digital techniques. Cadillac and Buick, for example, use analogue electronics and a simple logic chip in the Automatic Level Control for rear suspension. An Optron diode sensor measures the distance from the axle to the frame. Then, using the analogue and logic circuits, the system adds or subtracts compressed air in the shock absorbers to bring the car to the correct level.

In 1977, Oldsmobile and Delco-Remy used microprocessors in their MISAR spark control system. MISAR (Microprocessed Sensing and Automatic Regulation) senses crankshaft rotation, manifold vacuum and coolant temperature and decides which of more than 200 ignition advance points on a 'map' of possibilities suits the engine best at any particular moment. The points are stored in ROM and a Rockwell microprocessor is used. Other micros are used for other tasks. The Cadillac Tripmaster system, for example, uses a Motorola 6800 microprocessor to carry out navigational tasks. It handles time, distance and average speed calculations, and relates them to the rate of fuel consumption and the amount of fuel left in the tank.

It may be anticipated that combined analogue/digital devices will be replaced before long by solely digital controllers. United Technology has tested a digital injection computer, and Chrysler intends to use a similar device with its forthcoming Electronic Fuel Metering system (employing microprocessors from RCA and Texas Instruments).

Ford's Electronic Engine Control, the EEC-II, is scheduled for introduction on 1979 models. EEC-II incorporates a 12-bit microprocessor supplied by both Toshiba and Texas Instruments. The initial version, EEC-I, controlled spark advance and exhaust-gas recirculation; EEC-II also controls the air-to-fuel ratio by incorporating an electronically-controlled Feedback Carburettor and a three-way catalyst system. EEC-II, though more powerful than EEC-I, is nearly half the size with the number of microcomputer parts reduced by a third.

A wide range of microprocessor products is being developed for incorporation in cars, though it is important to keep current micro usage in proportion (of some 26 electronic systems in 1978 cars, only four used microprocessors for production models). One restricting factor is the lack of accurate, low-cost sensors. However, the trend is unmistakable. It is reliably predicted that by

1985 microprocessor systems will heavily outweigh the analogue-system equivalents for car applications.

Today particular microprocessors are being marketed for particular purposes. Intel is promoting the 8048/8049 and 8095 systems for use as engine controllers, claimed to be able to handle table look-up and to interpolate routines at the speeds necessary in a spark control or fuel-injection system. High-performance fuel and ignition controls still tend to be multichip applications, with many car manufacturers using standard TMS-9900 products.

The 1978 microprocessor-based systems are seen as a prelude to a mass micro invasion gaining momentum by the 1980s. The tougher exhaust emission and economy standards will put a premium on effective control of car functions, particularly in the US (with the rest of the world following), and this suggests encouragement for chip usage. Microprocessors may be expected to control all main engines variables, such as spark timing, choke control, fuel preparation, and fuel/air mixture supervision. In addition there will be the more frivolous applications such as radio and cassette-player control.

One estimate is that microprocessors worth an annual $1000 million might be required in the 1980s by the world's car manufacturers, with British firms having to order from abroad. It is suggested that Britain's requirement for car microprocessors might exceed an annual $10 million-worth, a quantity unlikely to be made available by UK chip makers. The Department of Industry and NEDC are working out plans to help national semiconductor manufacturers to meet the industrial needs of the future. There have been talks with Leyland to ascertain likely microprocessor requirements.

AEROSPACE

A substantial number of microelectronic developments have been stimulated by requirements in aerospace applications. The first microprocessors derived, at least in part, from Fairchild's early work in this area. The 1978 Farnborough aerospace exhibition saw an increased range of microprocessor-based systems, and the trend will continue. For example, the Ferranti Argus M700 minicomputer, designed for military applications, is a reimplementation of the 700 using AMD2901 bit-slice microprocessors. It includes a floating point processor and is assembled on two standard Euro-cards. The M700 has a very efficient Coral 66 compiler and the Mascot real-time executive.

Another Farnborough exhibit was the International Aeradio Stratus voice switching and control system for air traffic and other command and control applications. The system is based on Z80 microprocessors, and use is also made of 8048 single-chip microcomputer for decoding of multiplexed signals and for switching.

Microprocessors are now becoming standard components in aircraft, military rockets and space probes. It is suggested that modern aircraft are becoming so complex that it will soon be impossible to fly them without computer assistance. In one projected scenario, all cockpit instruments of the future will be replaced by a VDU screen. The on-board microcomputer will flash information to the pilot via the screen, with safeguards to prevent the pilot making errors. The computer may freeze the controls if the pilot takes a wrong decision and tries to act on it.

(In an experiment, conducted by Sem-Jacobsen of the EEG Research Institute in Oslo, a microprocessor-based system has been used to record and process brain activity in divers working in the North Sea.)

Rockets and space probes require a facility for rapid and efficient manipulation of digital data. There is also the requirement that on-board computing capacity be light and small. It is essential to minimise the mass of the projectile and so to minimise fuel requirements and associated costs. Microcomputers are essential components for applications in the aerospace environment.

PRINTING AND PRINTERS

Microprocessors are influencing both the character of the printing industry (the generation of traditional hard-copy material such as magazines and newspapers) and the character of specialised printers designed for particular purposes in a computer environment (eg to provide digital or word output on continuous stationery).

The effect of microprocessors on typesetting is dramatic, and a source of concern to many people employed in the printing and newspaper industries. Not only can many printing operations now be automated, with the consequence that jobs are either greatly modified or abolished altogether, but there is at the same time less emphasis on the 'hard-copy' storage of information. If data is held in a computer file it can often be much more easily retrieved for display on a screen than can information in bulky paper files for scrutiny.

Printing used to be the sole method, apart from speech, of communication. It is now only a small part of an expanding communications industry. The last decade has seen a shift in the mix of different products produced by the printing industry. There will be greater changes in the future.

Design developments in the field of computer printers have usually been towards provision of greater intelligence, as with computer peripherals and terminals in general. One example is the range of microprocessor-controlled dot-matrix serial printers developed by Hewlett-Packard. The bidirectional printer can look ahead to detect spaces imbedded in the data stream: when 10 or more spaces between characters are discovered, the print head automatically accelerates at a rate of 45 ins/sec to the next printable character.

There is also provision for detecting and skipping leading and trailing spaces, with the head moving quickly to print the next material. There are three different printing modes in the 2631A printer (and in the 2635A printing terminal). The 2631A and 2635A operate under the control of an SOS microprocessor developed by the company. There are also such features as a fast-replacement cartridge ribbon, automatic underlining, and the sophisticated bidirectional facilities. There is also choice of character sets.

The IBM 3800 Printing Subsystem is also controlled by a high-speed microprocessor. The complexity of printer requirements led to the use of microprogrammed control logic so that hardware could be added or changed with little difficulty. The multilevel, interrupt-driven microprocessor is used to handle the control algorithms, the synchronization of events with the essentially asynchronous printer hardware, and the data and event rates.

In general, the 0.5 μS microprocessor controls the flow of data and control information to the printer. It also supervises the generation of electrophotographic print images at up to 20,000 lines per minute, places the images on paper, and controls the flow of paper to the output stackers. The use of a microprocessor in this application has allowed the introduction of a new range of facilities. The subsystem gives compatibility for user programs previously employed with impact printers. High standards of speed, quality and function are achieved.

PoS, CASH REGISTERS

In 1975 about a third of all cash registers in the US were electro-mechanical, a proportion that will have diminished to less than one per cent by the early 1980s. By that time, PoS (point-of-sale) and electronic cash register (ECR) devices will have saturated the market, most of the new electronic terminals simply replacing the old mechanical ones. The US annual changeover rate is estimated at between 150,000 to 200,000 units. Many of the new terminals are based on microprocessors.

Sheldon Industries, for example, is selling the Model 2000 based on a Motorola 6800 microprocessor. This ECR is capable of data collection. The company is also marketing a credit card reader and communications interface unit (the Model 1100) which will bring EFT (electronic funds transfer) capability to the 2000. The advent of microprocessors has encouraged the use of PoS terminals in US restaurants. Products are being marketed by NCR, Scan-Data and other companies.

The NCR 2160 terminal has a 10-line CRT, matrix printers, a pressure sensitive 119-key keyboard, and a microprocessor-based controller unit which can handle up to 16 terminals a mile away. COBOL programming is the norm. The 2160 tracks sales by terminal, department, cashier, etc, and checks inventory to the recipe level. This device is dubbed a 'fast food' terminal. At a later stage it will be developed for full restaurant applications.

The new families of PoS, cash registers, credit authorization terminals, etc, would not have been possible without micro-processors (see bibliography for market statistics).

EDUCATION

Microcomputers, purchased as commercial models or as ready-to-assemble kits, are finding an increasing range of applications in the classroom. They can be used to aid learning or instruction (CAL or CAI) in both computing and non-computing subjects, and they can be used to perform a variety of tasks in the school situation (eg time-tabling and test result analysis). Many schools and colleges have built up experience in using microcomputers. The devices are cheap enough to be within the budgets of most schools. Microcomputers are portable and small ('nonthreatening'), and students can get convenient 'hands-on' programming experience.

The University of California and Pasadena Polytechnic High School were two of the earliest users of microsystems in the educational environment. The US Computer Power and Light company is selling microcomputers specifically for school use. And it is not unknown for schoolwork to be organised for home computer systems. It is suggested that CAI requires little computing power with large memory facilities. One solution would be a microprocessor with video display and a memory module containing the course in question.

A major computer-based instruction facility is the PLATO Computer-based Instruction System at the University of Illinois, with simultaneous users numbered in the hundreds. The Hewlett-Packard and Digital Equipment timesharing systems, common in US schools and colleges, in total have thousands of users. The advent of personal computers, based on micros, will introduce a new dimension to education. In a relatively short time, millions of such devices will be in use in the home and in educational organisations. Qualitative changes in education may be expected.

Improvement in reliability has greatly increased the scope for personal computer usage in education. Microcomputers in the University of Michigan, for example, are being used in many classroom demonstrations: 1978 development projects focussed on preparation for laboratory sessions, information processing aids, and data generators for simulated laboratory activities. Libraries are seriously considering microcomputer usage on campus. Some music classes are using microcomputer systems for music analysis and synthesis, and for electronic music composition.

Learning about computers is a rapidly growing CAL area. Increased familiarity with computers allows teachers to use computers and their procedures as metaphors for other processes. Hence education about computers has relevance to education in general. The availability of cheap computing enhances the teacher's scope in many traditional education areas — simulation and gaming, problem-solving, creative activities, etc. An increasing percentage of schools in the US and elsewhere are using microcomputers to aid programmed learning, to throw light on the character of learning, and to assist classroom management.

Computers can automatically generate learning and testing materials. Computer-assisted test generation, easily handled on today's microcomputers, is already a popular tool in the classroom environment. Students in a mathematics course have used LOGO, a simple computer language, on a microcomputer to generate a mathematical system building from primitive elements. Micro-computers have simulated laboratories to explore student expectations. As another example, micros have been used to generate simple stories and poems, to facilitate the investigation of rules of language. These instances show how microcomputers can help in specific areas of instruction. It is hard to think of an educational field where micros are not already in use or potentially beneficial.

In one specific CAI application (Western Washington University), the CAI machine comprised microprocessor, a floppy disk and a video terminal. Work continues on the development of a Z80 and multiuser 6800 version, with experiments using a variety of CAI languages (including IBM Coursewriter, a variation of Coursewriter called CW3-WPL, and PILOT). In one view, PILOT/BASIC is the best composite CAI language, though it is possible to write courseware in whatever language is available. The aim in the project in question was to provide access to high-quality, tested, existing courseware at low cost.

In the UK, microcomputers are increasingly relevant to educational activity. Oundle School (Peterborough) uses a Motorola 6800 microcomputer system and also a Data General Nova. The school has been involved in computing since 1958, long before the birth of micros. At Eltham College, a Boys' school in South-East London, computing experience has been built up following the acquisition of four South West Telecommunications microcomputer kits. The equipment has been built up over a period and is now worth more than £10,000.

Particular computer kits are marketed specifically as training kits, particularly relevant to the school environment. For example, the Heath 6800-based ET-3400 Trainer is accompanied by the EE-3401 Microprocessor Course. There are 469 pages of theory in a programmed learning format, 255 pages of concurrent experiments, two audio cassettes (with a 230-page reference chart), and 130 pages of manufacturers' product information sheets. Other kits have their own particular features. The Scrumpi kit, for instance, has l.e.d. lamps to indicate the status of data lines, address lines and I/O lines. Memory is supplied in ROM and RAM. Another kit, the Mk14 from Science of Cambridge, is based on the National Semiconductor SC/MP. In late-1978, it retailed for about £40. Users are advised to choose their kits with care since no universal training scheme exists.

Some kits can be used for particular educational applications. One such kit, based on an Altair 8800 microcomputer, a Datum 5098 optical mark reader and a Texas Instruments 733 ASR keyboard terminal with dual magnetic tape cassettes, is used to construct a microcomputer-based test scoring system. The program is written in a subset of BASIC, handles 100 items per test, produces a single test score per person, and allows any number to be tested.

Another microcomputer application is the construction of timetables. Timetable problems can be investigated using micros. For example, a simple program has been used on a SWTPC 6800 microcomputer (*Personal Computer World,* October 1978, pp 62–66). Applications of this sort have both practical and educational uses. Students can be introduced to the timetabling problem and encouraged to work out how the microcomputer can be made to contribute to its solution.

In the future, there will be enhanced possibilities for communication between the learner and microcomputers. The micros will learn to recognise speech (see below) and gestures. Technological developments in the provision of database facilities for microcomputers will expand the potential for problem-solving and creative activity in machines. The ubiquity of the pocket calculator, unimagined a generation ago, indicates the future for microcomputers in their educational role. We may anticipate qualitative advances in educational practice, and light will be thrown on traditional controversies (eg, what do IQ tests measure?) when increased understanding of machine intelligence illuminates our appreciation of human potential. Microcomputers have unique contributions to make in these areas.

MEDICINE

There are many ways in which microcomputers have contributed in the fields of medicine and health. The sightless have been aided by modes of computer-assisted communication, and an application of microcomputers provides speech to those who have lost it through accident or cerebral palsy. It is expected that physiological measures will be incorporated as input, creating new facilities for people lacking the motor control necessary to operate typewriters or for speech.

Programmable keyboard and display combinations can be used to help speech-disabled persons to communicate. Researchers in nonverbal communication see microprocessors as making valuable contributions to programmable hardware that is easy for the handicapped to use. On one estimate there may be between 400,000 and 1.5 million users of equipment of this sort.

Most available items of hardware in this area consist of a keyboard, a cathode-ray-tube or alphanumeric display for viewing and editing, and (sometimes) a printer for producing a hard copy of the message. Typical devices are the Unicom (developed at the Massachusetts Institute of Technology), the TIC (Tufts Interactive Communicator, developed at the New England Medical Centre), and Autocom (developed for the Trace Research and Development Centre for the Severely Communicatively Handicapped). TIC, in its latest versions, is microprocessor-based. Messages created by the user are displayed on a 32-character display and typed on a strip printer. There are editing features, a two-page memory, and several specialized functions.

Autocom is also microprocessor-based and, wholly portable, can be attached to the arms of a wheelchair. It has display and strip printer, is user-programmable or can be programmed to the user's specification. It is expected that around 5000 such units may be sold in the US each year.

Microcomputers can also help in the field of prosthetics (artificial limbs). A major problem with prostheses has been the question of control. Electrical signals from muscles have been used to control artificial limbs, but the more degrees of freedom of the prosthesis (ie the more functional it is) the more complex must be the control signal from the muscles. However, the more muscles the prosthesis 'taps' for control the more cumbersome the device; and every amputee's stump varies as to the electrical signals available. Such problems can be solved using microcomputers.

Use can be made of a microcomputer-based function separation algorithm: finer detection of usable control signals can be achieved, allowing fewer electrodes. Parameter changes can be made, via software, to tailor each device to the individual using it.

There is even scope for helping quadriplegics to communicate using eye movements. Signals from the eye muscles are often the last area to be impaired in instances of neurological disease. At the University of Pennsylvania efforts are being made to develop a microcomputer-based educational and environmental control device for the severely handicapped using eye muscle movements as means of communication. As the user looks at a TV-typewriter display, the eye positions are digitised and fed to a microcomputer. In this way the user can give the machine answers to questions and tell it to turn on lights, to dial telephone numbers, to talk (if connected to a speech synthesiser), etc.

Another significant microcomputer application is in medical

diagnosis. A specific example is the Dioptron, a fully automated computerized instrument for measuring the objective refraction of the eye. The instrument, controlled by an Intel 4040 microprocessor, serves as an aid for the doctor. It can be used as little or as much as is required. The Dioptron automatic objective refractor controls firstly accommodation (focus of the eye from a distant object to a near point), and then records data to determine each eye's refractive error.

The microcomputer controls, via software, every activity of the instrument, ie every light operation, every switch-controlled action, and every signal to the stepping motors to move the lenses. The current version of the Instrument, Dioptron II, contains the microprocessor and other microcomputer elements on a single board, with a second board used for system components.

Medical applications of micros, though increasing in scope, still only account for about 3 per cent of all uses of microcomputers. A key medical use, as with Dioptron, is in handling data achieved through patient monitoring. For example, three different electrocardiogram (ECG) tracings can be electrically reduced to a single plot (termed a vectorcardiogram), a spatial summation of heart activity. Changes in VCG shape can be used to diagnose various heart conditions. Similarly, an electroencephalogram (EEG) can be processed in a microcomputer-based system for analysis of its frequency content.

A microcomputer-based device has been developed at the Massachusetts Institute of Technology to realize, simply by plugging in various modules, a range of medical instruments:

- cardiac output monitor;
- arrhythmia analysis monitor;
- portable EKG computer;
- vestibular function tester;
- regional blood flow monitor;
- pulmonary function tester;
- microwave radiometer.

Other instruments can be devised in this way, as required.

A wide range of patient-monitoring devices are now based on microcomputers. For example, a monitor developed in San Diego is contained inside one plug-in module for a standard physiological recorder. It can monitor bioelectric data and most of the important physiological parameters. A desk-top pulmonary function computer is preprogrammed with predictable normals, ensuing calculations taking into account age, sex, weight, etc. Another micro-based device monitors a person riding an exercise bicycle.

Microcomputers are being used to aid patient monitoring in intensive care units. One example is the use of a network of LSI-11 microcomputers at the Rotterdam Thorax Centre. Acutely ill patients are monitored by constant scrutiny of their condition: warnings are flashed to medical personnel whenever any health deterioration is detected. Another example is the employment of a SOL/20 Terminal computer in an intensive care nursery at the Children's Hospital Medical Centre (Northern California). Such facilities may be expected to become commonplace in hospitals of the future.

COMMUNICATIONS

The convergence of computing and communications as technology trends has long been apparent. In one categorisation they can both be conveniently subsumed under the broad class of information handling. It is to be expected that microcomputer usage will become increasingly important in the communications environment.

Microcomputers will gradually replace minicomputers in tele-processing and communications tasks. They will be used for specific new tasks, often to accomplish cost savings. For example, a microcomputer has been used to reduce connection times in a telephone network and so lead to an overall cut in time-sharing costs (*Computer Communication,* June 1978, pp 134–144). Microprocessors have also been used in distributed communications networks, and in the automation of discrete items of broadcasting equipment. The Scicon Demos system, a multiprocessor system based on a chain of microcomputers, is expected to have various communications applications.

Telecommunications systems are built up out of terminals, communication channels and switching equipment. The terminals generate control and data signals which are fed over the channels to the exchanges (switching equipment). The exchanges route the data after interpreting the control information. Processing is required at each stage of the operation, in the past provided by hard-wired logic or by minicomputers and mainframes. Today microcomputers can perform many of the necessary processing functions. For example, trunk circuits can be micro-controlled.

In applications where a mainframe computer has been used (eg in stored-program telephone exchanges), the work can now be allocated to individual microprocessors. Micros are thus used to control groups of lines or trunks, or to perform particular tasks such as path search for a complete system. In this way, processing power can be added on a modular basis as requirements increase. Furthermore, provision of relatively cheap back-up can improve reliability.

In application to protocols, one microprocessor might control an interface to a central processor, storing messages for access by other micros. A second microprocessor might handle the link to the packet switch network and multiplex several messages onto one network line. A third micro might handle the initial establishment of calls. An approach of this sort simplifies design and allows for trouble-free expansion.

Distributed computing power, based on microprocessing, is a useful approach in designing exchanges. Again there is the possibility of modular expansion and straightforward design. Trends of this sort may lead to 'home terminals' for professional communication with central office or other 'home-based' employees.

TERMINALS

Terminal and peripherals are relevant to a wide range of computer applications. Attention has already been given to PoS terminals using microcomputers, to printers, and to terminal usage in the communications environment. Some terminals (eg the Video-Composer self-contained single-terminal system) have a history and an identity by virtue of particular features, whereas other terminal facilities are less distinctive, acquiring significance more as contributing components in larger systems. The Microterm II disk-based CRT workstation, for example, is significant for being based on two Z80 microprocessors working in tandem on different tasks. The Microterm is intended for use in communications networks.

Terminals are now 'intelligent' by virtue of microprocessors. Local processing capability is enhanced and much of the computing load may be taken off the central processor to which the terminal is linked. Intelligent terminals and peripherals are now available in all the traditional areas, and such devices, formerly relying on relatively primitive hard-wired logic, are invariably microprocessor-based. For example, a wide range of data entry tasks can now be carried out by intelligent terminals. An RCA hand-held Micro-Terminal is based on the COSMAC CDP1802 microprocessor. It can interface directly with COSMAC hardware support systems, and can be readily designed into user-built systems to provide control, communications and debugging facilities.

Microprocessors and low-cost video chips have facilitated the production of a raster-scan video terminal, The Tektronix 4025, which combines in one package the functions of graphics and alphanumerics. One application is the creation of complex graphs. A virtual bit map has been developed for storing graphics data. Software allows the user to create a rectangular graphics region on the screen, with the rest of the display area becoming an alphanumeric region, The microprocessor then further divides the graphics region into cells, indicating to the host computer the size and location of the graphics region. The system offers flexibility of use.

In general, raster-scan displays using microprocessors offer low cost, easily refreshed, flicker-free images in colour or black-and-white. In design, the refresh memory is interfaced to the microprocessor. For a graphics display, interlaced memory can provide continuous refresh for dynamic RAMs. Another approach relies on hardware to map the refresh memory into a pair of registers.

Board-level graphics can be economic and effective. Plug-in boards can be purchased off-the-shelf to connect to popular buses. Boards usually interface with the Intel 8080 and Motorola 6800 microprocessors, and RAM, ROM and I/O can be added for system configuration. ROM-sited software will determine system capability.

Colour display facilities have been achieved in a number of terminal products. The Cromenco TV Dazzler, for example, consists of two Altair (S-100)-compatible boards linked via coaxial cable to a colour monitor. The Compucolor 8051 is a more recent example of a personal colour system. This is a complete computer system packaged in a cabinet, in total resembling a standard television receiver. The 8051 is equipped with a BASIC interpreter stored in ROM. Again system flexibility is enhanced by microprocessor facilities.

INSTRUMENTATION

Instrumentation is crucial in cars, certain types of data acquisition systems, medical equipment, etc. It is particularly important in the increasing range of computer-based laboratory hardware.

Microprocessors are being used to aid experimentation in scientific laboratories of all types. Experiments can be micro-controlled and instrumentation, essential to the accurate interpretation of results, can be micro-based. The Prosser Scientific Instruments 6100 anemometer, for example, uses a microprocessor to cut instrument characterisation and linearisation procedures from hours to minutes. In this way, the RCA 8-bit 1802 microprocessor helps to ease the task of measuring wind-tunnel turbulence. The 6100 development was backed by the Department of Trade and Industry, with software jointly developed by Prosser and Essex University.

The Tektronix 7L5 spectrum analyser is another device that benefits from microprocessor capabilities. Complex signal switching, formerly carried out by various mechanical and electronic provisions, is now organised by a microprocessor. This allows automatic optimisation of analyser functions. The incorporation of microprocessors in these sorts of devices has also led to improvements in modular instrumentation.

Another microprocessor-based device is the Fluke 8500A, originally introduced three years ago. This is a modular instrument system programmed to perform the functions of a multimeter. The controller module incorporates an Intel 8080 microprocessor, and creates 'virtual' modules by manipulating data from actual plug-in modules. The 8080 enhances the digital multimeter's scope.

Microprocessors also aid data acquisition and test work in the laboratory and factory environments. Micros have assisted collection and assessment of experimental data in a chemical research laboratory. (*Microprocessors*, June 1978, pp 139–145), and the use of microprocessors in test instrumentation has made instruments more versatile and also allowed complex test systems to work in a way that resembles the distributed control system on the plant floor.

Interface compatibility has been aided in various instrument applications by the development of the IEEE 488 Bus, termed by some the microcomputer interconnect system of the future. Use of the bus helps cut the level of investment in automatic test equipment, facilitating automation at much lower levels. The bus may be seen as particularly relevant to the needs of small automatic test set-ups in laboratories and factories.

The HP 3585A spectrum analyser uses a microprocessor, plus a synthesizer based on a new phase-locked loop, to improve the accuracy of amplitude measurements. The microprocessor provides ease-of-use, despite the 3585A's complexity and versatility. Display methods are improved. Micros have facilitated the use of small dedicated processors for image reconstruction and analysis. There are many advantages in using a microprocessor interfaced with standard television equipment in an automatic image analysis system. The benefits include cheapness, portability, flexibility, high reliability and low power consumption.

SPEECH SYNTHESIS, VOICE RECOGNITION

Microprocessor applications in these areas are relevant to teaching aids, telecommunications, use of terminals and peripherals, aid to the disabled, domestic products, etc. Products for speech synthesis and voice recognition have been available for some years, but only recently have they started to incorporate microprocessors.

The Speak and Spell speech synthesis circuit from Texas Instruments is based on a single P-channel MOS chip. Its purpose is to help children in the 7–12 age group learn how to pronounce more than 200 basic words that are often spelled wrongly. The machine pronounces each word randomly and the user keys in a spelling on the alphabetic keyboard. Speak and Spell responds either with praise or encouragement to try again. After a set of ten words it declares the user's score. The device teaches pronunciation by first displaying the word and then pausing to give the user a chance to say it out loud, before giving the correct pronunciation.

The system is based on the TMC 0280 synthesizer chip, the TMC 0350 ROM, and the TMC 0270 controller. When the system generates speech, the controller specifies to the synthesizer the starting point of data stored in the ROM. The 131,072-bit ROM holds around 165 words or 115 seconds of speech, depending on the data rate. ROM output provides the pitch, amplitude and filter parameters used by the synthesizer chip to construct the speech waveform. The microprocessor is based on the TMS1000 series and is used to control the system.

Speak and Spell is the best known of a number of products that talk. Votrax of Troy (Michigan) manufactures portable speech synthesizers for the vocally impaired. This company also makes a Business Communicator, able to translate up to 64 telephone Touch-Tone inputs into an audio response and to synthesize English and German (with plans for Spanish, Japanese, French and Persian).

Comutalker Consultants (California) sells a speech synthesizer that links to the S-100 bus. The user can manipulate nine control parameters directly, or an optional software package automatically computes the parameters from phonically spelled ASC11. Synthesis boards compatible with S-100 are also produced by Speech Technology (California), generating speech from stored vocabularies. Master Specialities (again California) produces a talking calculator, as does Telesensory Systems for the blind. The new chips are programmable.

Speech- and voice-recognition systems are increasingly based on microprocessors. Such systems have appeal to industrial and commercial users of computers. The Nippon Electric Company has produced a Voice Data-Input Terminal based on microprocessors. Threshold Technology (New Jersey) has been using the LSI-11 16-bit microcomputer in models since 1976. The Threshold and NEC models can recognise groups of words without pause. NEC uses a TTL pattern-matching processor, a high-speed bipolar assemblage used to match patterns of incoming speech with those in a reference memory. A 16-bit microcomputer provides overall system controls. The system can be expanded to recognise up to 400 words.

Speech recognition is sometimes distinguished from speech understanding: in the latter, stored knowledge can be used to check if the word sequences make sense. For example, a speech understanding system, using syntactical analysis, has been employed to input the moves of a chess player. Speech understanding systems can only be designed for a specific problem where the semantics are known.

GAMES AND DOMESTIC

Microprocessors are moving into the home for various purposes, sometimes without our knowledge. Home-sited computers may be hobby kits, used to produce personal computers. They may be 'invisible' devices incorporated in domestic appliances such as cookers, washing machines, dish-washers, sewing machines, etc. Or they may lurk in electronic games, plug-in television devices and toys.

According to one survey more than half the home computers bought in the US by hobbyists are used as sophisticated toys or as electronic television games. Other uses include teaching, controlling the central heating, and keeping track of household accounts and income-tax details. It is suggested that computers will reach 20 per cent of the general public by 1985. Personal computers are already used extensively in the business and office environments, and 'home' buyers have included estate agents (using Intel 8080s and BCL Molecular 18s). Whitegate, part of the Provident Financial Group, have used custom-built microprocessor-based systems to match property with likely buyers. Each unit comprises an Intel 8080 with four floppy disks and a Soroc VDU. The Molecular 18 systems are being developed for estate agents Frank Powell.

Airfix and Hornby, in the toy world, have introduced microprocessor train controllers, the various systems able to handle several locomotives at the same time. The engines carry chips which control the power being picked up from the track. Hornby's Zero 1 system has a keyboard on which codes corresponding to different trains can be tapped out. Both firms aim to launch these products in 1979.

There is a growing range of microprocessor-based video games and chess computers. Personal chess computers (eg Chess-Challenger and Boris) are acquiring increasingly sophisticated software: often several levels of skill are possible in one machine. Boris, for example, is based on the Fairchild F8 microprocessor and is programmed for all classic chess moves (eg castling, en passant, queening). It can also display a few chatty phrases. Chess competitions have been held for hobby computerists, competing amongst each other and against the commercial purpose-built machines.

Available microprocessor-based games include Master Mind, Tank Battle, versions of golf, games of chance (blackjack, poker dice), Battleships, and various 'numbers' games (in one of these the aim is to discover a number that has been randomly generated). Toys and games are seen as one of the significant growth areas for domestic microprocessor-based products. Some of the hobby applications are unusual. One man has used a micro kit to operate a pipe organ. In another application, an Altair 8800 has been combined with a pipe organ to produce a music system that can be adapted to other instruments. The possibilities are endless.

6   Social Consequences

INTRODUCTION

Computers in general and microprocessors in particular are having a great impact on developed society. There is some debate about the nature of this impact, but a broad consensus that the social effects of computing are profound. People do disagree on whether the effects are good or bad. Will microprocessors throw millions of workers into permanent unemployment, or relieve people from mundane and dangerous duties, freeing them for creative activity and leisure? The question bears on technology and politics. Once the character of the technological impact is understood, there is at least a chance that we will be able to influence the development of society.

A decade ago, before microprocessors had burst upon the scene, there was much speculation about the possible effect of computers on jobs. The then-chairman of the Prices and Incomes Board, Aubrey Jones, speculated – in concert with many other pundits – that perhaps computers would create 'technological unemployment'. The late-1978 report from the Advisory Council for Applied Research and Development (ACARD) commented that 'over the next 10 to 15 years there will be changes in both manufacturing and service industry which will affect the whole UK economy'. Efforts have been made – by government, trade unions, specialist computer bodies, etc – to clarify the issue, to indicate a proper basis for national policies in the light of technological trends.

There is some indication that worries about the impact of microprocessors on employment are peculiar to Europe: no anxiety was shown at the 1978 Anaheim National Computer Conference. Chambers of Sperry Univac argued that the first industrial revolution had provided freedom from poverty and that the second would provide freedom from drudgery. (About one page of his 292-page book, *Computer Technology: Impact on Management,* is devoted to 'loss of jobs through automation'.)

But other observers are less sanguine, more ready to admit that microelectronics and automation trends are adversely affecting employment in some countries. Technology moves fast and it is difficult for social institutions and political attitudes to adapt. At a Sperry Univac seminar, held in October 1978 at Nice, emphasis was given to the accelerating pace of technological change. Whatever social effects we have discerned so far are likely to be more evident, rather than less, in the future. Nor should the impact of non-computing technologies — for example, molecular biology and genetic engineering — be ignored.

Some social effects of microprocessors only relate indirectly to employment. In January 1979 the Microprocessor Specialist Group of the British Computer Society took part in the BCS '79 Living With Computers conference and exhibition. A central theme was the impact of microprocessors on life in general. There has been speculation on the effect of personal computer ownership, made possible by microprocessors, on individual attitudes (*Personal Computer World,* No. 2, 1978, pp 8—9): 'owners behave differently from users'. And Le Rapport Nora, an official French report on the computerisation of society, has examined possible effects on existing power structures and national independence.

Traditional areas of social concern that relate to computing — privacy, energy consumption, defence — have acquired a new urgency, partly because of the advent of microprocessors, partly for other reasons. Microprocessors are exciting because of the unprecedented applications challenge that they represent. At the same time, steps should be taken to avoid the areas of social dislocation — through unemployment, excessive police surveillance, etc — that micros might bring about. We are constantly being told that the choice is ours. First, we must understand the situation.

THE SOCIAL IMPACT

In one categorization (*Microprocessors,* June 1977, p 307), the impact areas for microprocessors are broadly identified as: work, health, education, public affairs, social life, leisure, travel and home. The impact on some of these areas has already been indicated in Chapter 5. It is possible to say more — particularly on work and employment — in the present chapter. And other issues are also important.

The size and relative cheapness of microprocessors make them very attractive as system components — in communications networks, traffic control, encryption for privacy protection, etc. Such usage may have dangers in some circumstances. Micros have sometimes been characterised as 'subtle and silent' devices, easily able to slip below the threshold of conscious attention. They could be incorporated in devices without the user knowing, performing functions that were unsuspected. Such considerations are clearly relevant to privacy, police activity, industrial espionage, etc.

In many commercial and industrial applications, microprocessors are being used to displace human skill. If human involvement in the process survives, ie if workers are not made redundant, then there are two options. Either the people are retrained to embrace new skills (eg programming) or they are given mundane jobs (eg straightforward machine-watching). The prevailing option depends upon a number of factors, eg the economics of the process, the philosophy of managers, the vigilance of unions. If work is 'de-skilled', there will be an inevitable loss of job satisfaction. This will affect employee attitudes to plans for the introduction of microprocessors (or larger computers) elsewhere in a plant. In such circumstances it is clearly in management interest to implement microprocessor-based systems with minimum disruption to the workforce, and with complementary plans for career development wherever this is possible.

The impact of microelectronics will also be felt by people working on the new technology. The emphasis in semiconductor research is changing: some of the basic physics problems have been solved and the current focus is very much on applications. A consequence is that the physicist is contributing less, proportionately, than formerly, and the same is true of the electronics engineer. Tasks previously tackled by custom-built integrated circuits can now be tackled by programming: the role of the software engineer is increasing.

There is also speculation about the possibilities in computer-aided design. It may well be that design techniques will be formalised to the point that they can be computerised. An application requirement will be rigorously defined and then the microcomputer will get on with the job of system design. It is also possible that micros will learn to generate their own programs, and software for other machines. Microprocessor developments will impinge on computer professionals, as well as on workers in other fields.

Microprocessors will eliminate many dangerous and unpleasant jobs. For example, paint-spraying, work with asbestos and the manufacture of certain chemicals are increasingly being auto-mated, partly for health considerations; and it is likely that robots will be designed to dispose of refuse, to clean out sewage tanks, and to perform other necessary tasks that may be aestheti-cally disagreeable. At the same time there will be an enhancement of micro applications in the home and in entertainment (briefly profiled in Chapter 5). Such developments — variously abolishing dangerous, unpleasant and mundane jobs, and enriching home and leisure activities — will profoundly affect lifestyles.

It may be easier to travel, with automated systems, but there may be less need to. It will be possible to work at home and to play at home, in relative isolation. Microprocessor-controlled holographic systems may make it possible to have a 'social' life, without coming into contact with human beings. Andy Warhol is supposed to have said that soon it will be possible to attend parties with just you there! Simulation systems will allow anyone to climb Everest, pilot Concorde and explore the surface of Mars. It may be possible to stimulate the pleasure centres of the brain directly, by means of programmed micro devices responding to biofeedback information.

At present these items are largely fanciful. There are practical questions of pressing importance to be considered. Central among these is the possible impact of microprocessors on employment.

THE EMPLOYMENT QUESTION

There is much uncertainty about the likely impact on employment of microelectronics in general and microprocessors in particular. Many articles are quick to point out the speculative nature of these considerations. At the same time there are plenty of clues as to what may happen.

The Swiss watch industry has been shattered by the manufacture of digital watches in the US. Seventeen Swiss firms have collapsed, resulting in widespread unemployment and the loss to the United States of a 200-million dollar industry. The clock industry in South West Germany has also slumped because of competition from electronic timepieces, resulting in an employment drop over a few years from 32,000 to 18,000. Many of the employees in the industry are now semiskilled machine operators. In one Swiss factory, 16 workers control 400 machines that cut teeth for watch parts. These are classic instances of the deskilling conse-quences of developments in microelectronics.

Similarly, in many other manufactured items electromechanical components have been replaced by silicon chips. One example is the elimination of mechanical moving parts in cash registers. This has led to National Cash Register, between 1970 and 1975 reducing its manufacturing workforce from 37,000 to 18,000.

American Telephone and Telegraph, who supply most telephone systems in North America, has reduced its manufacturing labour force from 39,200 in 1970 to 19,000 in 1976. Western Electric, the manufacturing part of AT & T, has estimated that a 75 per cent reduction is also feasible in the labour required for fault-finding, maintenance, repair and installation work. The telephone equipment companies in Europe are faced with the same problem. In the UK a 30 per cent reduction in jobs in this area has been seen between 1976 and 1979. Similar trends are evident in super-market chains, the clothes industry, offices, fabrication plant, design houses and elsewhere. (These points are highlighted in the much quoted article by Colin Hines – *The Chips are Down*, published by Earth Resources Research Ltd, 40 James St., W1.)

Over recent decades the textile industry has experienced vast technological development: over a 23-year period labour productivity rose 314 per cent, with UK jobs falling from 581,200 in 1971 to 479,000 in 1976. One reason for the reduction in jobs was the declining share of the world market. Another reason was technical innovation. For example, productivity is enhanced by the computer-controlled double jacquard knitting machine which cuts the time needed to change a pattern from 3–4 hours to a few minutes. Another innovation is the electric mill-monitoring system which allows a single weaver to supervise a large number of looms without reducing cloth quality.

In the banking sector, largely because of the introduction of computers, employment fell from 315,600 in 1971 to 263,000 in 1976. The move towards automated services for customers will further reduce the number of workers needed in the banking industry. Similar trends can be seen in the office environment with the introduction of such devices as word processors. In a West German study carried out by Siemens it is suggested that by 1990 nearly a half of present office work could be carried out by computerised equipment, threatening the jobs of 2 million of West Germany's 5 million typists and secretaries.

In February 1979 the Bradford branch of NALGO was involved in a dispute about the impact of microprocessor-based word processors. It was claimed that 18 or 19 copy typists' jobs were lost when Word-Plex equipment came on stream in June 1977. In November 1978 NALGO rejected plans to instal a word processor in the Bradford education department, fearing that another 90 jobs might be lost. (The Bradford dispute came at a time when the National Enterprise Board was announcing investment plans for NEXOS, a subsidiary to coordinate the development of British office systems in conjunction with Logica. The NEB had already set up INMOS to develop chip hardware and INSAC for software.) The problems at *The Times* also indicate possible industrial relations difficulties caused by microprocessor-based systems.

Design activity is increasingly being turned over to computers. A microprocessor can design a kitchen in minutes, where formerly up to ten hours would be required. A software package called PDMS is being used to design pipe layouts for process control contractors. Three-dimensional representations are constructed of every item of plant, down to the level of flanges and gaskets. The user can specify the view he wants from any angle for graphics display, and component data can be recalled for materials costing and ordering. Computerisation is increasingly significant in the design of aircraft, cars, weapon-systems, municipal schemes, medical equipment, etc. The activities of skilled design engineers will more and more be threatened by the efforts of automated systems.

A microprocessor is used to control a driverless vehicle intended for distributing goods and mail in offices, hospitals, industrial complexes, etc. The vehicle travels along programmed routes, stopping at predetermined positions. Hotels, restaurants and hospitals can be managed, at least in part, by microprocessor-based systems. And microprocessors can supervise flame-cutting machines, warehousing, wiring assembly design, cheese manufacture, hot powder forging, chemical flow in pipelines, power generation, etc. The consequences for work and employment, in many disparate areas, are likely to be profound.

One writer (I. Clark, *Computing*, 6/7/78, pp 14–15) has coined the word 'robomania' to denote 'an exaggerated affection for mechanisms which mimic human activity' (perhaps 'robophilia' would have been a better term). He scrutinises the idea that people can effectively be replaced by machines. The speculative points have been largely outflanked by the event. Automated systems are clearly replacing human beings in many applications. In this circumstance there are many conflicting estimates of the consequences for employment. One typical estimate is that there will be between three and five million people unemployed in the UK by the 1990s.

Trade unions and government are responding in various ways in this situation (see below). On the whole unions are resisting the simple Luddite reaction (though it is interesting to see how frequently the words 'Luddite' and 'Luddism' are appearing in discussion of the problem). Professor Michie of the Machine Intelligence Unit at Edinburgh University has pointed out that Luddism 'never yet turned back the industrial clock'. At the same time, perhaps the Luddites, like the suffragettes, forced discussion of the important issues. Ian Benson of TASS has emphasised that, though the Luddites were defeated in their efforts to prevent the spread of the factory system, they did influence the widening of the franchise, the formation of trade unions, and the regulation of conditions of employment.

The TUC has become increasingly concerned at the impact of microelectronics. In 1965 it could declare that mass unemployment was caused through inadequate economic and social policies, rather than through technological change. Now the Manpower Services Commission is saying that there will be a shortfall of jobs of 2.3 million by 1981. This sort of estimate is forcing the TUC and other bodies to scrutinise the impact of technology, and in particular the impact of microelectronics. At the 1978 TUC conference, Bryan Stanley, of the Post Office Engineering Union, declared that unionists should not be 'latterday Luddites, blindly opposing all changes in technology and insisting on the maintenance of existing equipment and skills however inefficient, however irrelevant they become'. Emphasis was given to the role of the unions in focussing attention on the human and social implications. David Basnet, the TUC chairman, pointed out that technology could bring opportunities as well as difficulties. Here, government has a prime responsibility.

THE GOVERNMENT RESPONSE

Governments have to appear optimistic and positive. They can only highlight problems if they point to solutions. If they appear negative, doom-laden and confused they will not last long. The government in the UK, in common with governments elsewhere, has tried to cultivate an optimistic view of microelectronics and is investing heavily in micro production, application and education.

Emphasis has been given to how microprocessors can improve efficiency in commercial and industrial processes, and how new

jobs will derive from developments in the microelectronics industry. Ben Bova, the science fiction writer, has suggested (*Computer
Weekly*, 5/10/78, pp 10–11) that the computer revolution will
increase work rather than leisure by freeing people from repetitive
tasks for more original work. Another idea is to create more jobs
by the use of particular financial devices, eg to reduce the cost of
labour as a factor in production, thus stimulating demand, at the
same time implementing labour subsidies paid by expenditure
taxes (*Computer Weekly*, 19/10/78, p. 22).

In Britain, the Employment Minister Albert Booth has remained
'enormously optimistic' that the microprocessor revolution will
prove to be of great benefit to the country. He has pointed to the
partnership between organised labour and government as giving
hope that the problems will be overcome, at the same time
acknowledging that many people see the microprocessor trends
much in the way that 'the Luddites saw new machinery – as a
threat to jobs rather than as a means of satisfying social needs
and building up employment opportunities'.

One idea is that people will move from manufacturing to
service industries. (Manpower Services Commission figures indicate
that over the last decade there has been a reduction of one million
in those working in manufacturing, and an increase of one million
among those working in services.) Some observers have suggested
that this idea is difficult to reconcile with political plans (in all
parties) to restrain or reduce public expenditure. Albert Booth
has also suggested that the current obsession with the 'micro
revolution' may be just the 'latest mode or fashion'. At any rate,
it is argued, there is no justification for widespread gloom.

At the 1978 TASS conference (see *Computer Technology and
Employment*, 1979, jointly published by NCC and TASS), Albert
Booth gave various reasons for optimism about microelectronic
trends. Micros will lead to a saving of raw materials, especially the
fossil fuels, and they should help the American car industry to
achieve the current targets for exhaust emission. Microprocessors,
like plastics before them, may well stimulate a vast new range of
products, so stimulating the demand for labour. There will, for
example, be a requirement in the motor industry for devices
devoted to route-finding, creating potential for employment of a
new kind.

In some commercial and industrial areas, microprocessors are
more likely to fill gaps than to create redundancies. And in any
event more unemployment will be created in the long run by

ignoring technological trends than by implementing developments rapidly and with confidence.

Various union leaders have suggested how the government should approach the question of technological innovation. Ian Benson, for example, one of the most active trade unionists in this debate, has proposed more effective government planning and a restructuring of education and training institutions (*Computer Weekly*, 2/11/78, p 4).

The UK government, like other governments, has responded to the microprocessor challenge with a range of investment plans. In mid-1978, plans of the National Enterprise Board to set up a UK semiconductor company for the manufacture of dynamic RAMs sparked off vigorous debate. Some experts suggested that the market would be too competitive while others suggested that it would be large enough to absorb total world production.

Part of the plan was to establish a wafer fabrication facility to produce 64K RAMs. Money would also be invested in assembly and test equipment, and in research and development. Some of the INMOS research and development activity will take place in the US and some production will be sited in the Far East, INMOS is attracting specialist staff to its UK operations.

Another central plank of the UK government's microprocessor scheme is the Microprocessor Application Project (MAP) scheme, first announced in 1978. MAP covers three areas:

— *training and courses,* handled by The National Computing Centre in conjunction with the Department of Industry. £2 million originally allocated in this area to maximise 'industry awareness';

— *feasibility studies,* carried out by authorised consultants and controlled by Warren Spring Laboratory. £3 million originally allocated to this area, with individual firms able to obtain up to £2000 for studies into the use of micros in processes or end-products;

— *project funding.* £10 million originally allocated.

By late-1978, nearly 2000 enquiries had been received by companies wanting more information about project funding, and about 50 specific projects had been put forward for funding. The applications being considered for funding include a wide range of processes and products, eg weighing machines, transport, machine tools, instruments, agricultural equipment, chemicals, textiles, vending machines, games, etc.

About 300 companies have so far responded to the invitation to be authorised consultants for the feasibility study part of MAP and the list is now closed. The main condition for inclusion in the MAP-consultants list (Mapcon) is that the applicant must have successfully completed a microprocessor project. The procedure is that a company wishing to develop a micro-based project is directed to an authorised consultant who will carry out a feasibility study, later being able to recover up to £2000 of the cost of the study. One central MAP aim is to reach engineering firms with little or no experience of microprocessor technology.

In December 1978, the government announced further plans to assist microprocessor developments in this country. In a joint memorandum from three Ministers (the Secretaries for Industry, Education and Employment) the government outlined its plans to the National Economic Council. Part of the memorandum is reiteration of piecemeal announcements over the last six months. There is also a detailed examination of education requirements (which will take £60 million). A further £40 million was allocated to boost the various MAP activities.

The memorandum emphasises that industry must be willing to invest, and that people must be willing to retrain and if necessary move to new jobs. The government acknowledges its responsibility to provide adequate protection, compensation and incentive for workers who need to retrain and move.

In early 1979, the State's stake in microelectronics was more than £400 million. This figure approaches the Japanese investment and exceeds that in France and Germany. The British tax-payers' involvement is now running at about £250 million, to which should be added NEB project-assistance, aid to GEC (for its chip-manufacturing venture with Fairchild), and other assistance funding. Part of the government's policy in this area follows the September 1978 report (*The Applications of Semiconductor Technology*) from ACARD (the Advisory Council for Applied Research and Development).

There is inevitable debate about whether the government plans will succeed. Doom-mongers are not hard to find. Plenty of observers suggest that INMOS will not be able to compete with the large established US companies, or with the Japanese. The Council for Educational Technology has pointed out the 'desperate urgency' of the situation, and has opted (late-1978) for a gloomy view: 'Some might argue that the suggested major social change may not happen . . . jobs will be created, the present level of unemployment will be seen as nothing more than a short-term aberration. Perhaps so: but all the indications are otherwise'. Peter Large (*Guardian*, 8/12/78) quoted the yokel giving directions to a lost motorist: 'If I were you I wouldn't start from here'.

It may be that the pessimists are exaggerating the grimness of the future. There is a natural sluggishness, not only in Britain but elsewhere, in implementing new technology. It is not usual commercial or industrial practice to implement immediately a new technique becomes feasible. Society may have time to accommodate to the inevitable changes that will come about. But in circumstances where many experts see more microelectronic developments in the next twenty years than in the last we can scarcely be complacent.

THE UNION ROLE

In 1956 and 1957 the TUC focussed attention on the effect of automation on non-manual workers. During the 1956 congress it was declared 'that the effect of mechanisation on clerical employees might be greater than on manual workers'. The 1957 congress report identified two emerging schools of thought. One suggested that the benefits of automation should go to the workers operating it, leading to reduced hours worked, longer holidays, and higher rates of pay. The other proposed greater producitivity and lowering of prices. The report concluded that fears of redundancy among clerical workers were probably exaggerated. Advice was given to assist unions when considering automation in offices — 'The controlled introduction of mechanisation into office work should be welcomed on the assumption that a) the community as a whole benefit by improved living standards and b) full consultation and negotiation will take place at all stages and levels in order to safeguard the interests of members'. These proposals, scarcely Luddite, are pertinent in the current microprocessor situation.

In 1963 the TUC surveyed the effects of computerisation on office staff, and repeated the survey in 1969. The 1970 annual report could declare that 'the introduction of the computer did not appear to have resulted in any overall decrease in staff'. The computer impact on employment was not thought at that time to be a troublesome matter. Displacement of labour had occurred, but for other reasons. Issues that were of concern related to personal privacy and the trade union use of computers.

The TUC's attitude to the Younger Committee findings on privacy were reported in 1973. It was argued that Younger had paid insufficient attention to employment data processing and storage, and to the control of data banks. There was concern also that unions themselves were not using computers for their own purposes. This view was reiterated at the 1978 TASS conference where it was proposed that computer retrieval of relevant information could strengthen the hand of trade unions in pressing claims and arguing for particular industrial policies.

The employment issue has come to the fore again with the emergence of microprocessors and their undoubted impact on the job scene. Some unions, with long involvement with computers, have made particular efforts to monitor developments. APEX (the Association of Professional, Executive, Clerical and Computer Staffs), for example, has set up a working party to look at word processors, to assess the impact on jobs and the possible effects of VDUs on health and safety. Some traditional union strength will be weakened simply through increased redundancies reducing union membership. One call is that people in particular jobs and professions should be unionised quickly, before their jobs disappear. It is recognised that with the development of microprocessors, diagnostic software, custom-built packages, etc, even certain types of data processing jobs – programmers, electronics engineers, etc – will be affected.

In September 1978 the TUC debated a notion that focussed specifically on the microelectronics issue. Microelectronics were seen as posing 'both a challenge and a threat to members', with concern expressed that 'insufficient is being done by Government either to exploit the new opportunities or to evaluate the employment consequences of the developing technology' (this was before the December government announcement of considerable additional aid to MAP and other schemes). In the motion the General Council is urged to press the government to initiate discussions with the TUC on steps necessary to ensure:

— the establishment or development of a substantial indigenous UK manufacturing capacity for microprocessors and associated computer systems;

— the provision of sufficient trained manpower to meet the manufacturing requirements of both hardware and software;

— an evaluation of the employment consequences of microelectronics;

– forward planning, at both national and plant level, to ensure the maintenance and, if possible, the expansion of employment levels against the background of these developments.

The microprocessor impact was also debated in depth at the 1978 TASS conference on the effects of computer technology on employment. An edited version of the full conference proceedings is published jointly by NCC and TASS (*Computer Technology and Employment*, 1979). A speech by Albert Booth, Minister of Employment, is included with important supporting papers.

Many points (sometimes conflicting) were made at the TASS conference (reference should be made to the NCC/TASS book). One significant suggestion was that workers should be retrained to move into developing technology fields. This proposal was also made at the September 1978 Joint International Seminar on the Teaching of Computer Science, sponsored by IBM and held at Newcastle University.

Professor K. Nygaard, of the Norwegian Computing Centre, has been closely involved with the Norwegian Federation of Trades Unions on the formulation of an agreement with the national employers' federation on the introduction of computer-based systems. At the Newcastle seminar he declared that over the next few years a major retraining of systems designers will be needed to meet the demands of trades unions that members be involved at all stages of design and implementation of new computer systems. A Norwegian agreement was signed in 1975, expressing the right of employees to be fully informed of plans to introduce computer technology as soon as the first decision has been taken, and before systems design has begun. Similar legislation is planned in Sweden and Denmark, and it may be anticipated in the UK within a few years. Any reading of the literature indicates that unions have resisted discernible Luddite pressures (letters to *The Morning Star* notwithstanding). The unions are pressing for consultation and involvement, prepared to respond to realistic government initiatives.

The outcome of the policies and attitudes cannot be predicted with any confidence. Crystal-ball gazing is a hazardous occupation. (A prestigious predictive scientific report in the 1930s managed to miss out nuclear power, the jet engine, and computers!) We can influence developments but a number of important factors are outside our control. Perhaps Britain has noticed microprocessors rather late in the day, but in 1978 the microelectronic chip received UK government recognition. We have started to do what is necessary, and there is a comforting doctrine that beginnings are always a good thing.

Bibliography

Chapter 1

Leventhal L A, Semiconductor Technologies and Semiconductor Memories, *Simulation,* August 1976, pp 65–71.

Microcomputer Components, *Mini-Micro Systems,* Nov–Dec 1977, pp 50–51, 54–58.

Ogdin C A, Microcomputer Storage Media, *Mini-Micro Systems,* January 1978, pp 34–35, 38, 40, 43–44, 46.

Gates Arrays Taking Over in Logic Using ECL, *Electronics,* 30/3/78, pp 39–40.

Know a Microcomputer's Bus Structure, *Electronic Design,* 21/6/78, pp 78–84.

Handle Microcomputer I/O Efficiently, *Electronic Design,* 21/6/78, pp 70–76.

Kewney G, Electron Beams for Making Microcircuits, *New Scientist,* 22/6/78, pp 815–817.

Russell D, Microprocessor System Partitioning, *Microprocessors,* Vol. 2, No. 3, June 1978, pp 147–149.

Alexandridas N A, Bit-Sliced Microprocessor Architecture, *Computer,* June 1978, pp 56–80.

Ogdin C A, Microcomputer Buses – Part I, *Mini-Micro Systems,* June 1978, pp 97–100, 102, 104.

Santoni A, Sapphire Ribbons Bring the Cost of CMOS/SOS Circuits Way Down, *Electronic Design,* 19/7/78, pp 36, 39.

Force G, Microprocessor Bus Standard Could Cure Designers' Woes, *Electronics,* 20/7/78, pp 113–118.

Ogdin C A, Microcomputer Buses – Part II, *Mini-Micro Systems,* July 1978, pp 76–78, 80.

Aspinall D, Microprocessor, Memory and Input/Output Structures, *Microprocessors*, Vol. 2, No. 4, August 1978, pp 231–234.

Bursky D, 16-Bit µPs to Offer Performance, Address Range, Data Paths of Minis, *Electronic Design*, Vol. 26, No. 18, 1/9/78 pp 46–48, 50.

Bursky D, Support Getting Stronger as uPs Advance to 16-Bit Level, *Electronic Design*, Vol. 26, No. 18, 1/9/78, pp 66–67, 70.

Gregg P, Who's Missing the Bus Then? *Electronics Weekly*, No. 947, 15/11/78, p 2.

Forbes B E, IEEE 488: A Proposed Microcomputer I/O Bus Standard, *Computer Design*, November 1978, pp 170, 172, 174.

Sutton P, Microcomputer Architecture – An Introduction, *Personal Computer World*, December 1978, pp 16–18.

Voakes P, Silicon is Plentiful – But There's Not Much on Sale, *Electronics Times*, 25/1/79, pp 6–7.

The Shrinking World of Electronic Chips, *Design Engineering*, January 1979, pp 12–13.

Whitworth I, Review of Microprocessor Architecture, *Microprocessors and Microsystems*, January/February 1979, pp 21–28

Capece R P, Faster, Lower-Power TTL Looks for Work, *Electronics*, 1/2/79, pp 88–89.

Blood, W R, High Density Raises Sights of ECL Design, *Electronics*, 1/2/79, pp 99–107.

Jacobs J, C-MOS on Sapphire Sparks Small Computer's Performance, *Electronics*, 1/2/79, pp 108–113.

Wilkins C, Putting the Bits Together, *Datalink*, 19/2/79, pp 8–9.

Chapter 2

Toshiba Markets Japan's First 8-Bit Microprocessor Chip, *Electronics*, 2/9/76, pp 5E–6E.

Ferranti's Micro Opportunity, *Mini-Micro Monitor*, 22/9/76, pp 1–2.

Colin A, Intel 3000 and AM 2900 Microprocessors – A Comparison, *Microprocessors*, June 1977, pp 287–292.

Coll J, Direct Addressing: Where to Get Your Personal Computer, *Personal Computer World*, February 1978, pp 55–58.

Smith Ivor, Microprocessor System Design, *Microprocessors,* February 1978, pp 3–10.

Wiles M, et al, Compatibility Cures Growing Pains of Microcomputer Family, *Electronics,* 2/2/78, pp 95–103.

Russell D, Microprocessor Survey, *Microprocessors,* February 1978, pp 13–20.

Microcomputer Systems, *NCC Computer Hardware Record,* April 1978.

Comparison Charts, *Microprocessors,* April 1978, pp 96–101.

Microsystems Launched at the Fair, *Computer Products International,* May 1978, p 7.

Milton R, Product Review – Microprocessors, *Computer Products International,* May 1978, pp 8, 10–17.

Morse, S P, et al, The Intel 8086 Microprocessor: A 16-Bit Evolution of the 8080, *Computer,* June 1978, pp 18–27.

Powers I, MC6809 Microprocessor, *Microprocessors,* June 1978, pp 162–163.

Kornstein H, 8086 – Its Development and Capability, *Microprocessors,* June 1978, pp 166–169.

Pearce C A, The HP-67 and HP-97 – Hewlett-Packard's Personal Computers, *Byte,* June 1978, pp 112–117.

Frenzel L, How to Choose a Microprocessor, *Byte,* July 1978, pp 124–132, 134–136, 138–139.

Tyeti C A, Terminate Your System for Life, *Personal Computing,* pp 67–73.

Harrison N, A Guided Tour of the Z80, *Personal Computer World,* July 1978, pp 48–51.

Ittner W F and Miller J A, Microcomputer's On-Chip Functions Ease Users' Programming Chores, *Electronics,* 20/7/78, pp 129–133.

One Apple Which Grew Without Giving Anyone the Pip, *Practical Computing,* July/August 1978, pp 12–13.

Peuto B L and Prosenko G J, One-Chip Microcomputer Excels in I/O – and Memory-Intensive Uses, *Electronics,* 31/8/78, pp 128–133.

Zilog Z8000: An Architectural Overview, *Microprocessors and Microsystems,* August 1978, pp 242–244.

Knottek N, Mini and Microcomputer Survey, *Datamation,* August 1978, pp 113–114, 116–118, 120, 122–123, 126.

Nelson P, The Number Crunching Processor, *Byte,* August 1978, pp 64–68, 70, 72, 74.

Bond J, The 16-Bit 8086, *Mini-Micro Systems,* August 1978, pp 86–87.

Adams W T and Smith S M, How Bit-slice Families Compare: Part 1, Evaluating Processor Elements, *Electronics,* 3/8/78, pp 91–98.

Kehoe L, Latest 16-Bit MPU Secrets Revealed, *Electronics Weekly,* 20/9/78, p 13.

Davy B, Advanced Intelligence, *Personal Computer World,* September 1978, pp 39–40.

Computing's Fun With Your Pet, *Practical Computing,* October 1973, pp 21–24.

Tandy Review, *Practical Computing,* November 1978, pp 21–23, 36–37, 39.

Microprocessor Data Manual II, *Electronic Design,* 11/10/78, 90 pp.

Introducing the Nearest Thing to a Single Chip: the 8022, *Microprocessors and Microsystems,* October 1978, pp 295–297.

Update on Fairchild, *Microprocessors and Microsystems,* October 1978, pp 298–299.

Update on Zilog, *Microprocessors and Microsystems,* October 1978, pp 300–301.

Firebaugh M et al, A Feast of Microcomputers, *Personal Computing,* November 1978, pp 60–70.

Barnes D, Bursky D, 8-Bit-Compatible or Mini-Like, 16-Bit 1-Board µCs Do More Faster, *Electronic Design,* 23/11/78, pp 30, 34, 36.

Wiess G G, The Total Software Upward/Downward Compatible R65XX Microcomputer Family, *Euromicro Journal,* January 1979, pp 7–10.

Ritter T, Boney J, A Microprocessor for the Revolution: the 6809, *Byte,* January 1979, pp 14–16, 18, 20, 24, 26, 28, 30, 32, 34, 36, 38, 40, 42.

Winder, R O, Microprocessor Code Compactness, *Microprocessors and Microsystems,* January/February 1979, pp 9–13.

Dixon T M, More on the 8086, *Personal Computer World*, February 1979, pp 25–27.

Micro Firm Chips Away at Rivals, *New Scientist*, 1/3/79, p 675.

Microcomputer Development Systems, *NCC Computer Hardware Record*, March 1979.

Small Business Computer Systems, *NCC Computer Hardware Record*, June 1979.

Chapter 3

Aspinall D and Dagless E L (editors), *Introduction to Microprocessors*, Pitman, 1977.

Hardware/Software Tradeoff, *Mini-Micro Systems*, November – December 1977, pp 98–103, 106.

Vittera J F, Handling Multilevel Subroutines and Interrupts in Microcomputers, *Computer Design*, January 1978, pp 109–115.

Coll J A, A Look at Available Microcomputer Hardware and Software, *Computer Education*, February 1978, pp 18–20.

Dowsing, R D, Software Support, Part 2 High-Level Languages, *Microprocessors*, February 1978, pp 42–43.

Bass C, PLZ: A Family of System Programming Languages for Microprocessors, *Computer*, March 1978, pp 34–39.

Salisbury A B, Structured Software for Personal Computing, *Creative Computing*, March/April 1978, pp 58–64.

Bushell R G, Higher Level Languages for Microprogramming, *Euromicro Journal*, 4, 1978, pp 67–75.

McKendry, M S, The Use of Monitors in Microprocessor Software Development, *Euromicro Journal*, 4, 1978, pp 257–264.

Gallacher J and Wakefield P, Software Organization of a Microcomputer-Based Data-Acquisition System, *Microprocessors*, April 1978, pp 59–64.

Dowsing R D, An Introduction to Structured Programming, *Microprocessors*, April 1978, pp 88–89.

Bowies, K L, UCSD PASCAL: A (Nearly) Machine Independent Software System, *Byte*, May 1978, pp 46, 170–173.

CIS COBOL, *Computing*, 11/5/78, p 17.

Magers C S, Managing Software Development in Microprocessor Projects, *Computer*, June 1978, pp 34–42.

Rauscher T C, A Unified Approach to Microcomputer Software Development, *Computer,* June 1978, pp 44–54.

Patterson W and Frisbie K, Reduce Your µC System's Overhead, *Electronic Design,* 7/6/78, pp 122–124.

Hughes P, Factoring in Software Costs Avoids Red Ink in Microprocessor Projects, *Electronics,* 22/6/78, pp 126–130.

Schindler M J, Fit Your µC With the Right Software Package, *Electronic Design,* 5/7/78, pp 64–72.

Powers W M, Microprogram Assemblers for Bit-Slice Microprocessors, *Computer,* July 1978, pp 108–120.

Rooney M, Develop µP Software Efficiently, *Electronic Design,* 19/7/78, pp 62–65.

Ready-to-Run Software is Coming Here Fast, *Practical Computing,* July/August 1978, p 14.

PASCAL – 6 articles, *Byte,* August 1978, p 49.

Weems C, Designing Structured Programs, *Byte,* August 1978, pp 143–154.

Saunders J L and Lewis L E, High-Level Languages Ease Microcomputer Programming, *Electronics,* 3/8/78, pp 115–118.

Hearn A D, Some Words About Program Structure, *Byte,* September 1978, pp 68–70, 72, 74–76.

High-Level Languages, The Next Technology, *Microprocessors,* October 1978, pp 286–289.

Coll J, BASIC: Interpreter or Compiler? *Microprocessors,* October 1978, pp 289–291.

Hemenway J, The 8080 Gets a "Full-Blown" FORTRAN, *Mini-Micro Systems,* October 1978, pp 78–80.

Ferguson D F and Gibbons A J, A High-Level Microcomputer Language, *Mini-Micro Systems,* October 1978, pp 90, 92–93.

Microcomputer Software, *Update,* November 1978, pp 8–9.

Hemenway E and Hemenway J, Z80 COBOL – A Big League Language in a Little Machine, *Mini-Micro Systems,* November 1978, pp 86, 88–89.

Off-the Shelf Packages for Pet, *Practical Computing,* December 1978, p 36.

Meinzer K, IPS, An Unorthodox High Level Language, *Byte,* January 1979, pp 146, 148–152, 154, 156, 158–159.

Maurer W D, An Introduction to BNF, *Byte,* January 1979, pp 116, 118, 120, 122, 124–125.

Sherertz D D, An Exposure to MUMPS, *Byte,* January 1979, pp 74, 76, 78, 80, 82.

Lloyd M, Costing Microprocessor Software, *Microprocessors and Microsystems,* January/February 1979, pp 29–31.

Whitbread M, Software Development and System Testing Techniques, *Microprocessors and Microsystems,* January/February 1979, pp 15–18.

Caudill P, Using Assembly Coding to Optimize High-Level Language Programs, *Electronics,* 1/2/79, pp 121–124.

Chapter 4

Shelton C, Microprocessors Offer Free Bonuses for the Designer, *Engineering,* March 1976, pp 179–182.

Stein P, When Should You Use a Microprocessor? *Computer Decisions,* April 1976, p 18.

Designers Need and Are Getting Plenty of Help, *Electronics,* 15/4/76, pp 116–117, 120–122.

Queyssac D, System Design Considerations, *Electronics Weekly,* 21/7/76, p 6.

Hnatek E R, Microprocessor Device Reliability, *Microprocessors,* June 1977, pp 299–303.

Hardware/Software Tradeoff, *Mini-Micro Systems,* November/December 1977, pp 98–103, 106.

Implementation and Checkout, *Mini-Micro Systems,* November/December 1977, pp 108–116.

Santoni A, Low-Cost Automatic Testing Makes Cents – But Not All the Time, *Electronic Design,* 6/12/77, pp 30, 32.

Santoni A, The Latest Logic Analyzers Offer More Functions and Less Cost, *Electronic Design,* 1/2/78, pp 26–28, 30, 32.

Comley R A, Error Detection and Correction for Memories, *Microprocessors,* February 1978, pp 29–33.

Foose R, Module Minimises Repair Time of Process-Control Systems, *Electronics,* 2/3/78, pp 121–124.

Adams G and Rolander T, Design Motivations for Multiple Processor Microcomputer Systems, *Computer Design*, March 1978, pp 81–89.

Scrupski S E, Why and How Users Test Microprocessing, *Electronics*, 2/3/78, pp 97–104.

Castleman K R, The Intelligent Memory Block, Adding Processors to Enhance Performance, *Byte*, March 1978, pp 186–192.

Rozsa K, Multiprocessing Boosts Microcomputer, *Electronic Design*, 15/3/78, pp 72–75.

Del Corso D, An Experimental Multimicroprocessor System With Improved Internal Communication Facilities, *Euromicro Journal*, 4, 1978, pp 326–332.

Laszlo Z and Arato P, Microprogrammed Logic Network Design, *Microprocessors*, April 1978, pp 73–76.

Farrell E P and Kanellopoulos N G, Debugging Aids for Microprocessor Systems, *Microprocessors*, April 1978, pp 83–87.

Fielland G and Oishi K, Keep the Memory Interface Simple, *Electronic Design*, 26/4/78, pp 84–92.

How to Test Microprocessors and Microprocessor Products – A Good Question Looking for Answers, *Electronic Design*, 10/5/78, pp 75–77.

Kewney G, Microprocessors Don't Always Work, *New Scientist*, 18/5/78, pp 454–455.

Bisset S, LSI Tester Gets Microprocessors to Generate Their Own Test Patterns, *Electronics*, 25/5/78, pp 141–145.

LeBoss B, Switch to Micros Has Them Sweating, *Electronics*, 25/5/78, pp 89–90.

Magers C S, Managing Software Development in Microprocessor Projects, *Computer*, June 1978, pp 34–42.

Rauscher T G, A Unified Approach to Microcomputer Software Development, *Computer*, June 1978, pp 44–54.

Ogdin C A, Microcomputer Buses, *Mini-Micro Systems*, June 1978, pp 97–100, 102, 104.

Cosserat D, The True Costs of Microprocessing, *Microprocessors*, June 1978, pp 115–118.

Purkiss N, Microprocessors – Engineers Face Some Testing Demands, *Electronics Weekly*, 14/6/78, pp 24–25.

Burzio G, Operating Systems Enhance Microprocessors, *Electronic Design*, 21/6/78, pp 94–99.

Hughes P, Factoring in Software Costs Avoids Red Ink in Microprocessor Projects, *Electronics*, 22/6/78, pp 126–130.

Conway J C, Hardware Approaches to Microprogramming With Bipolar Microprocessors, *Computer Design*, August 1978, pp 83–91.

Webster R, How Micros Will Change the Face of Computer Design, *Computer Weekly*, 7/9/78, p 15.

Stakem P H, Weigh Hardware and Software Options to Optimize Your Microprocessor Design Solutions, *Electronic Design*, 13/9/78, pp 106–110.

Smith K, British Work on Multimicro Systems, *Electronics*, 14/9/78 pp 92–93.

Whitbread M, Design Techniques With Microprocessors, *Microprocessors*, October 1978, pp 263–267.

Palya W L, Configuring an LSI-11 System, *Mini-Micro Systems*, October 1978, pp 63–68.

McDermott J, Distributed Microprocessor Systems Advance Process-Control Designs, *Electronic Design*, 11/10/78, pp 34, 36.

Lyman J, LSI Boards Give Testers Fits, *Electronics*, 23/11/78, pp 91–92.

Williams E, The Pros and Cons of Microprocessor Plan, *Engineer*, 12/10/78, pp 48–49.

Dennis M, Things You Wanted to Know About Micro's But Were Afraid to Ask – Hints on System Design, *Personal Computer World*, December 1978, pp 21–23.

Bently A W, Microcomputer Development System Offers Adaptable Test Configurations, *Computer Design*, December 1978, pp 122, 124, 127–128.

Robach C, et al, Microprocessor Systems Testing – A Review and Future Prospects, *Euromicro Journal*, January 1979, pp 31–37.

Lowe L, Designing for Testability, *Microprocessors and Microsystems*, January/February 1979, pp 3–6.

Gladstone B E, Comparing Microcomputer Development System Capabilities, *Computer Design*, February 1979, pp 83–90.

Chapter 5

Seim T A, Microprocessors Aid Experimentation in Scientific Laboratory, *Computer Design,* September 1976, pp 83–89.

Hatch R I, Microprocessor Multiplies a Digital Multimeter's Functions, *Electronics,* 16/9/76, pp 97–101.

Fenton R W and Hollom J H, Exploring the Advantages of Microprocessor Usage, *Electronics Weekly,* 22/9/76, pp 11, 13.

Minis, Micros and CAI, *Journal of Computer-Based Instruction,* May 1977, pp 5, 103–128.

Li K, Microprocessor-Based Video Games, *Electronic Design,* 6/12/77, pp 84–87.

Muller D, Personal Computers in Home and Business Applications, *Computers and People,* December 1977, pp 11–12, 20, 27.

Macdonald A, Intelligent Terminal "Softcopy" Forms Eliminate Paper Chase, *Irish Computer,* January 1978, pp 14–15, 18.

Emery T M, The Evolution of a Computer Terminal, *Mini-Micro Systems,* January 1978, pp 48, 50.

Microprocessors, *Euromicro Newsletter,* January 1978, pp 4–26, 39–52.

Findlay G I et al, Control of the IBM 3800 Printing Subsystem, *IBM Journal of Research and Development,* January 1978, pp 2–13.

Micros Rival Minis at School, *Computing,* 9/2/78, p 25.

Matic B and Trottier L, Graphics CRT Displays are Easy, *Electronic Design,* 15/2/78, p 68–73.

Brown F, MPUs Make the Mark on VDUs, *Electronics Weekly,* 15/2/78, p 2.

Wind Tunnel Linearization is a Breeze When a Microprocessor Comes Along to Help, *Electronics,* 16/2/78, pp 6E, 9E.

Burkett A, Industry Starting to Take Micros Away From Their Parents, *Engineer,* 16/2/78, pp 64–65.

Gilder C, MPUs and Highways Presage the Future, *Electronics Weekly,* 22/2/78, p 6.

Steinwedel J, Personal Computers in a Distributed Communications Network, *Byte,* February 1978, pp 80–82, 94, 96, 98, 100–101.

Heesbeen E, LSI-11 Microcomputers in Hospital ICU's, *Interface Age,* February 1978, pp 68–71.

Baker F B et al, A Microcomputer Based Test Scoring System, *Educational Technology,* February 1978, pp 36–39.

MUSE and Microcomputers, *Computer Education,* February 1978, pp 9–24.

Kellock B, The Microprocessor Revolution Hots-Up, *Machinery,* 1/3/78, pp 25–27.

Lederer J H et al, A Two Computer Music System, *Byte,* March 1978, pp 8–10, 12, 48, 50, 52–54.

Marathe A D and Chandra A K, Hardware/Software for Process Control I/O, *Computer Design,* March 1978, pp 122, 124–126.

Olson H, Controlling the Real World, *Byte,* March 1978, pp 174–177.

Single-Board Microcomputers Monitor and Control Hydroelectric Plant With Remote Supervision, *Computer Design,* March 1978, pp 64, 66, 68–69.

Crow F C, Shaded Computer Graphics in the Entertainment Industry, *Computer,* March 1978, pp 11–22.

Raskin J, The Microcomputer and the Pipe Organ, *Byte,* March 1978, pp 56, 58, 60, 62, 64, 66, 68.

Foose R, Module Minimizes Repair Time of Process-Control Systems, *Electronics,* 2/3/78, pp 121–125.

Burkitt A, Bleak Outlook for Microprocessors in the Motor Industry, *Engineer,* 23/3/78.

First Micro Chess Champs, *Computing,* 6/4/78, p 12.

Seybold J W, The Versatile VideoComposer, *Seybold Report,* 10/4/78, pp 3–12.

Voice Recognition Unit for Data Processing Can Handle 120 Words, *Electronics,* 13/4/78, pp 69–70.

Astrop A, Getting a Feel for Minis and Micros, *Machinery,* 19/4/78, pp 66–68.

Davies J, How Microprocessors Simplify and Extend Future of NC Machines, *Engineer,* 27/4/78, pp S19, S22–S23.

Gibbs J and Temple R, Frequency Domain Yields Its Data to Phase-Locked Synthesizer, *Electronics,* 27/4/78, pp 107–113.

Toner M C et al, Automatic Image Analyser, *Microprocessors*, April 1978, pp 90, 92–93.

Microcomputer Control's Eyes Focus and Measures Refractive Error, *Computer Design*, April 1978, pp 64, 68, 72.

Bradbeer R, Microcomputer Kit Review, *Microprocessors*, April 1978, pp 78, 80–81.

Leventhal L A, Microprocessors in Aerospace Applications, *Simulation*, April 1978, pp 111–115.

White J S, White Collar Microcomputers, *Interface Age*, April 1978, pp 39–40.

Dozier G W, A Plentiful Harvest, *Personal Computing*, April 1978, pp 57–63, 66–70.

Rwzic, N P, The Automated Factory – A Dream Coming True, *Control Engineering*, April 1978, pp 58–62.

Single-Chip Microcomputer as a Petrol Pump Controller, *Measurement and Control*, April 1978, p 125.

Boxer S M and Batchelor B G, Microprocessor Arrays for Pattern Recognition, *IEE Journal of Computers and Digital Techniques*, May 1978, pp 60–66.

Gann S O, Chips With Everything, *Datalink*, 8/5/78, pp 8–9.

Defence Electronics, *Electronics Weekly*, 10/5/78, pp 11–14.

Johnston R, A Typewriter in Your Pocket, *Computer Weekly*, 11/5/78, p 4.

Dozier H W and Green R S, *Electronics*, 11/5/78, pp 105–110.

Kerr J, Robot Welders are All Set to Make Giant Strides in Britain, *Engineer*, 11/5/78, pp 32–33.

MPUs Will Give Process Control Bigger Boom Than in Late 1960s, *Electronics Weekly*, 24/5/78, p 11.

Williams E and Burkitt A, Master Microprocessors, *Engineer*, 25/5/78, pp 42–43, 45, 47.

Le Boss B, Switch to Micros Has Them Sweating, *Electronics*, 25/5/78, pp 89–90.

PoS in the Restaurants . . . Coming Into Its Own At Last, *Autotransactions Industry Report*, 29/5/78, pp 1–2.

Microprocessor Controls Fastener Tension, *Design Engineering*, May 1978, p 33.

Dwyer T A and Critchfield M, Colour Graphics on the Compucolour 8051, *Byte,* May 1978, pp 32–36, 38–39.

Georgiou B, Give an Ear to Your Computer, *Byte,* June 1978, pp 56–58, 60, 62, 64, 66, 68, 70, 72, 74, 76, 78, 80, 82, 84, 86, 88, 90–91.

Personal Computers for Business, *EDP Analyzer,* June 1978, pp 1–13.

Newhouse S, Contract Fulfillment, *Personal Computing,* June 1978, pp 28–42.

Miller-Kirkpatrick J, Build Your Own Computer, *Data Processing,* June 1978, pp 42, 45, 48.

Smith I, Microcomputer System in a Communications Environment, *Computer Communications,* June 1978, pp 139–145.

Stewart K and Littler J S, Graphics-Oriented Data Collection Unit, *Microprocessors,* June 1978, pp 139–145.

Computers in Industrial Control, *Control Engineering,* June 1978, pp 49–51, 53–54, 56–58, 61–64, 66–67, 69–71.

Tennant H, Natural Language Processing and Small Systems, *Byte,* June 1978, pp 38, 40, 42, 44, 46–48, 50, 52, 54.

Norton W H, Notes on Teaching With Microcomputers, *Byte,* June 1978, pp 138–139.

Rippiner H, Graphics Meet Data, *Electronics Weekly,* 7/6/78, p 13.

Hamilton P, Communicators Help the Handicapped, *Electronics,* 8/6/78, pp 94, 96–97.

Cane A, Soldering On With Curry's Chips, *Computing,* 8/6/78, p 19.

Woolnough R, Motorola Hits MPU Jackpot, *Electronics Weekly,* 14/6/78, p 1.

Scicon and NPL Develop System Based on Micros, *Computer Weekly,* 29/6/78, p 3.

Chapman D, Chips With Everything, *Printing World,* 6/7/78, pp 12–13.

Bodley N, Here's A Breakthrough – A Low-Cost Speech Synthesizer on a Chip, *Electronic Design,* 19/7/78, p 32.

Green D A and Meers J, MPU Could Lead to "The Office at Home", *Electronics Weekly,* 19/7/78, p 16.

McDermott J, and µC-based Control Systems Cut Engine Pollution, Up Mileage, *Electronic Design,* 19/7/78, pp 20–22, 24, 26.

Klein A, Microprocessors Continue to Add Versatility to New Test Instrumentation, *Control Engineering,* July 1978, pp 41–42.

Goff R C A, The Bedside Microcomputer in the Intensive Care Nursery, *Interface Age,* July 1978, pp 64–67.

Moberg D, Medical Applications of Microcomputers, *Interface Age,* July 1978, pp 76–79.

Kessler E, Production Recording for Profit, *Production Engineering,* July 1978, pp 44–47.

Using SWTP Micro System at Eltham College, *Practical Computing,* July/August 1978, pp 8–11.

Driving Into a Micro Sunrise, *Computing,* 3/8/78, pp 14–15.

1977 Sparked 20% PoS Industry Growth, Says IDC . . . And the Pace Will Continue, *Autotransactions Industry Report,* 7/8/78, pp 1–5.

Wiggins R and Brantingham L, Three-Chip System Synthesizes Human Speech, *Electronics,* 31/8/78, pp 109–116.

Adams W T and Smith S M, Postscript on Bit-Slice Families: Microcontrollers Serve Many Needs, *Electronics,* 31/8/78, pp 138–139.

Groupe D et al, A Microprocessor System for Multifunctional Control of Upper-Limb Prostheses via Myoelectric Signal Identification, *IEEE Transactions on Automatic Control,* August 1978, pp 538–544.

Allen S A and Rossetti T, On Building a Light-Seeking Robot Mechanism, *Byte,* August 1978, pp 24–26, 28, 30, 32–33, 36, 38, 40–42.

Microcomputers, *Datamation,* August 1978, 19 pp.

Micros Get CNC Costs Under Control, *Machinery,* 20/9/78, pp 79–82.

Williams E, It's All Systems Go for Vaughan as Move to Diversify Pays Off, *Engineer,* 21/9/78, pp 36–37.

Chip In, Everybody, *Economist,* 23/9/78, pp 91–92.

Zinn K L, A Place for Personal Computing in Schools and Colleges, *Interface Age,* September 1978, pp 70–75.

Production Processes Monitored by Microprocessor Controlled Noncontact Inspection Systems, *Computer Design,* September 1978, pp 55, 58, 62, 64, 66.

Micro-Based Games and Calculators, *Computer Weekly,* 5/10/78, pp 13–17.

Sweeten C, Timetabling for Schools, *Personal Computer World,* October 1978, pp 62–66.

Gibbons J, Micros or Calculators? *Practical Computing,* October 1978, pp 17, 19.

Lynch G, Taking the Chore out of VAT, *Practical Computing,* October 1978, pp 59–62.

The Micro Master, *Practical Computing,* October 1978, pp 32–34.

McDermott J, Distributed μP Systems Advance Process-Control Designs, *Electronic Design,* 11/10/78, pp 34, 36.

Hubin W N, Heath Microprocessor Training System, *Byte,* November 1978, pp 158–159.

Micros That Are Made to Measure, *Machinery,* 8/11/78, pp 43–44.

Otsuka W, Microprocessor Makes Alphanumeric Display Smart, *Electronics,* 7/12/78, pp 137–141.

Seagrave J R and G, Opening New Worlds for Physically Handicapped, *Practical Computing,* January 1979, pp 59–90.

Sheppard D, Working with Microprocessors – MPUs Make Good DLS Supervisors, *Electronics Weekly,* 10/1/79, p 6.

Karstad K, Thurlow L, Working With Microprocessors – MPU Controls Real-Time Clock, *Electronics Weekly,* 17/1/79, pp 6, 18.

Boothroyd D, Chip Will Invade the Kitchen – Eventually, *Electronic Times,* 18/1/79, pp 14–15.

Wasmeier M, Speech Recognition and Speech Synthesis, *Euromicro Journal,* January 1979, pp 40–43.

Marovac N, Microcomputers in Computer Science Programmes, *Computer Journal,* February 1979, pp 91–94.

Summers M K, Microprocessors in the Curriculum and the Classroom, *Computer Education,* February 1979, pp 9–14.

The Ubiquitous Chip, *Printing World,* 1/2/79, pp 6–7.

Gosch J, Milling Machine Makes Small Lots of PC Boards, *Electronics*, 1/2/79, pp 5E–6E.

Chapter 6

Laver M, Microprocessors, Side Effects and Society, *Microprocessors*, June 1977, pp 305–308.

Gregory D, Rebecca and the Computer: The Trade Union Attitude to Data Processing, *Computer Bulletin*, December 1977, pp 6–7.

Ringer W V, Power to the People, *Personal Computer World*, February 1978, pp 8–9.

Benson I, Can Computer Staff Save Britain? *Computer Weekly*, 4/5/78, p 4.

Automation (8 articles), *New Scientist*, 8/6/78, pp 648–650, 652–666.

Brown F and Elliott M, NEB's Plunge: Sink or Swim? *Electronics Weekly*, 21/6/78, p 2.

NEB Sums Right for RAMs Project, *Computer Weekly*, 22/6/78, p 11.

Burkitt A, Training Industry to Use Microprocessors, *Engineer*, 29/6/78, p 11.

Michie D, Beware SCUM – The Society for Cutting Up Machine-Makers, *Computer Weekly*, 29/6/78, p 2.

Bailey R, Semiconductor Industry Report States Options, *Electronics Weekly*, 5/7/78, p 2.

Brown F, MPU Techniques to Get £5m DoI Boost, *Electronics Weekly*, 12/7/78, p 5.

Burkitt A, Whitehall Backs Its Enthusiasm by Cash for Micro Projects, *Engineer*, 13/7/78, p 33.

Lamond F, Nora Report – An Example of Open Government for the British to Follow, *Computer Weekly*, 13/7/78, p 18.

Grillet A, Impact of Understanding, *Electronics Weekly*, 19/7/78, p 15.

'Bleak Future' for Micro Applications, *Computer Weekly*, 20/7/78, p 19.

The Three Wise Men of Inmos, *Europa Report*, 14/8/78, pp 1–2.

Folberth O G, Impact of Very-Large-Scale Integration on Systems and People, *Computers and Digital Techniques*, August 1978, pp 69–73.

Cockroft D, How Micros Could Change the Role of the Unions, *Computer Weekly*, 31/8/78, p 4.

Dwyer J, Gloomy View of Six Wise Men, *Electronics Weekly*, 27/9/78, p 2.

The Applications of Semiconductor Technology, Advisory Council for Applied Research and Development, September 1978.

Webster R, A Revolution That Will Leave People Free to do Original Work, *Computer Weekly*, 5/10/78, pp 10–11.

Peltu M, Minister Optimistic on Jobs – But It's an 'Act of Faith', *Computer Weekly*, 12/10/78, p 14.

Cane A, Facing Up to the Future, *Computing*, 12/10/78, pp 16–17.

Beacon G, How to Create More Jobs Without Inflation, *Computer Weekly*, 19/10/78, p 22.

Key Holes for Training and Public Ownership, *Computer Weekly*, 2/11/78, p 4.

Race J, BCS Group Assesses the Impact of the Micro, *Computer Weekly*, 2/11/78, p 15.

Schwartz M, Wood R, Problems of Planning for Microelectronics, *Electronics Times*, 30/11/78, p 14.

Peltu M, Micro Fears Blur the Way Ahead, *Computer Weekly*, 25/1/79, p 2.

Gray J, UK's Salvation is in Micro Revolution, Jim Tells TUC, *Electronics Times*, 25/1/79, p 1.

Elliot M, Fears and Hopes of the MPU Revolution, *Electronics Weekly*, 31/1/79, p 5.

Laurie P, Britain Takes a Silicon Gamble, *New Scientist*, 15/2/79, pp 470–473.

Chips Go Down, *New Society*, 15/2/79, pp 358–359.

Computer Technology and Employment, NCC and TASS, February 1979.

Boothroyd D, Inmos Under Way – Top Design Team Hired by Denver, *Electronics Times*, 1/2/79, p 1.

Murphy J, DoI's £½ Million Grant Doubles Micro Training Programme in the UK, *Electronics Times*, 1/2/79, p 4.

The Devil Will Take the Hindmost, *Computing*, 15/2/79, pp 16–17.

Kewney G, Micro Centre for Every College, Report Urges, *Computing*, 15/2/79, p 1.

McLean M, Tony Benn — Contemplating the Division of the Rewards of the Micro Revolution, *Electronics Times*, 15/2/79, pp 12–13.

Unions Accept Microelectronics, *New Scientist*, 8/3/79, p 750.

Large P, UK Chips Need Shake-up, *Guardian*, 16/3/79, p 14.

Glossary

Access time	— The time taken to reference an item in storage, eg to read from or write to a memory location (see also Cycle time).
Accumulator	— A dedicated storage location, within the processor, containing data to be operated on.
Address	— A number or reference denoting a memory location containing data or a program instruction.
Address bus	— A physical connection between the microprocessor, memory, and other parts of the microcomputer.
Algorithm	— A set of rules for performing a task or solving a mathematical problem. Derives from the name of a 9th century Arab mathematician (Al Khwarizmi).
Alphanumeric	— Characters based on both letters and numerals (and often arithmetic signs, punctuation marks, etc).
Analogue	— A way of representing quantities in terms of proportionate physical quantities such as current or length. Usually contrasted with digital.
AND	— A logical operator. Contrasted with the arithmetic operators (add, subtract, etc). In binary, an AND circuit produces a 1 only when all the inputs are 1s.

Application   — What a computer does (eg traffic control or inventory management).

Application program   — A program (or software package) which carries out a required function

Architecture   — The way a computer is designed. The way its internal components are organised and interconnected.

Arithmetic and Logic Unit (ALU) — The circuit within the microprocessor that performs the logic and arithmetic operations.

Arithmetic shift   — Movement of each bit in an accumulator one position to the left or right.

Assembler   — A program which decodes assembly code into machine-readable code. Assembly code sets out instructions by means of mnemonics and is contrasted with binary machine code.

BCD   — Binary Coded Decimal. Each digit of a decimal number is translated into a binary equivalent (eg 23 becomes 010 011, contrasted with 10111 when the complete decimal quantity 23 is converted into binary).

Benchmark   — A set of test problems designed to allow the performances of different computers to be compared.

Binary   — An arithmetic system using base 2 (instead of, eg, base 10 in decimal arithmetic). The usual arithmetic system in digital computers.

Bipolar   — Semiconductor devices where the gain is obtained by interaction of positive and negative charge carriers.

Bit   — Binary digit (a 1 or 0).

Bubble memory   — Solid-state method of data storage in which bits are represented by small magnetic domains (bubbles), typically 3 micros in diameter.

Bus	— A physical connection between the internal parts of a computer. S-100 and SS-50 are the most popular microcomputer bus structures.
Byte	— A number or word comprising several bits. Often synonymous with character. The smallest unit with real meaning.
CCD	— Charge Coupled Device. A device in which information is stored by means of packets of small electrical charges.
Chip	— A piece of silicon, usually about a quarter of an inch square, carrying components which make up all or part of a microcomputer.
Clock	— Circuit which generates control signals to coordinate and initiate the various computer activities. Determines the speed of the computer.
Compiler	— A program that translates the user-oriented language into machine language, ie it translates the source program into code the computer can understand.
CPU	— Central Processing Unit. ALU plus registers and other components. Carries out logic and arithmetic functions, and supplies control signals.
CRT	— Cathode Ray Tube. Used to provide visual displays in terminals.
Cycle time	— Total time for a program instruction to reference a memory location, read from or write to it, and then return to the next instruction (see also Access time).
Data	— Information which is processed or stored by a computer. Data is to computers what information is to people.

Debug	– To remove (hardware or software) errors from a system.
Diagnostic	– A program or procedure used to detect faults. Reference to medical diagnosis using computers.
Digital	– A way of representing quantities in terms of digits. Usually contrasted with analogue.
Disk	– Means of storing data on magnetic material coating a circular metal plate. Uses concentric tracks. Floppy disks are flexible. Some disks are removable, some are not.
DMA	– Direct Memory Access. Means of transferring data between memory and peripherals without using the CPU.
EAROM	– Electrically-Alterable Read-Only Memory. Often a synonym for EPROM.
EPROM	– Erasable Programmable Read-Only Memory. Needs an erasing device that uses ultra-violet light.
Erasable memory	– Storage in which data can be written, erased and rewritten. Core, tape and disk are erasable.
Executive	– Software which provides control functions. Often a synonym for operating system.
Exorcizer	– Motorola development package for the M6800. Includes pretested modules.
Firmware	– A hardwired program. Essentially software fixed in ROM.
Flag	– A bit (or several) which says something about a piece of data. Can govern program jumps
Floppy disk	– A flexible storage medium (see also Disk).

Hardware — The various mechanical, electrical, electronic and magnetic parts of a computer. Contrasted with software.

Input/Output devices — The devices used to get information into and out of a computer. A typical example is the CRT terminal.

Language — The means used by a programmer to communicate with a computer. A low-level language is close to what the computer can directly understand. A high-level language is user-oriented (sometimes resembling English).

Mainframe — A large computer having wide range of facilities. Some confusion because people are also talking about microcomputer mainframes.

Memory — The data storage facilities. In microcomputers there are RAM, ROM, PROM, etc.

Microcomputer — A computer realised on a small number of silicon chips. A few microcomputers are based on only one chip.

Microprocessor — A CPU on a silicon chip. Included as part of a microcomputer.

Minicompputer — Middle-range computer, between mainframe and microcomputer. Some micros are now out-performing minis.

MOS — Metal Oxide Semiconductor. The common technology for integrated circuit manufacture.

Multiaccess — A system allowing several operators to use the same computer at the same time.

Multiprocessing — Division of programming tasks between several independent CPUs.

N-channel MOS   — A type of metal-oxide-silicon field-effect transistor using electrons to conduct current in the semiconductor channel.

NC machine tool   — A program-controlled device for cutting metal.

Nonvolatile memory   — Memory allowing preservation of data storage during power loss or system shutdown.

Object program   — The binary form of a source program. Produced by assembler or compiler, and understandable by the computer.

Operand   — Quantity involved in or resulting from the execution of a computer instruction.

P-channel MOS   — A type of metal-oxide-silicon field-effect transistor using holes to conduct current in the semiconductor channel.

Peripheral   — Device used with a computer to display or store data. Can be used to convert data to a form usable by the computer. Typical peripherals are printers, keyboards, graphics devices, etc.

Program   — A sequence of instructions to be followed by the computer.

PROM   — Programmable Read-Only Memory. A memory into which data can be written. No alterations allowed thereafter.

RAM   — Random Access Memory. Usable for computations and other program-controlled activities.

Register   — Element for temporary storage of data. Can be accumulators, address registers, instruction register, etc.

Resident software	— Programs incorporated with a proto-typing system to help user program writing and development.
ROM	— Read Only Memory. Usable for permanent storage of program or other data.
Semiconductor	— A material, usually silicon or germanium, which can be arranged as insulator or conductor.
Software	— All the computer programs associated with a computer system.
Source program	— A program (not written in machine language) which is translated by assembler or compiler.
Static memory	— A type of semiconductor read/write RAM not requiring refresh cycles.
Subroutine	— A group of instructions reached from more than one place in a main program.
Terminal	— A device allowing communication between a computer and an operator some distance away. Similar to a peripheral.
Timesharing	— A system in which CPU time and system resources are shared between a number of tasks.
Transistor-transistor logic (TTL or T^2L)	— Integrated-circuit logic in which the multiple inputs on gates are provided by multiple emitter transistors.
Volatile memory	— Read/write memory whose content is lost when electrical power is removed.
Unipolar	— Transistors formed from a single type of semiconductor material, either n-channel or p-channel, as used in field-effect transistors.

Wafer (or slice)   — A thin disk of semiconductor mat-
                            erial in which many devices are
                            fabricated at the same time. Wafers
                            are later assembled together.

Word   — A set of bits handled as a primary
                            unit of information. Hardware design
                            determines the length of the com-
                            puter word.

Index